WALKING IN LANCASHIRE

Printed in Singapore by KHL using responsibly sourced paper

A catalogue record for this book is available from the British Library.
All photographs are by the author unless otherwise stated.

Updates to this Guide

While every effort is made by our authors to ensure the accuracy of guide-books as they go to print, changes can occur during the lifetime of an edition. This guidebook was researched and written before and during the COVID-19 pandemic. While we are not aware of any significant changes to routes or facilities at the time of printing, it is likely that the current situation will give rise to more changes than would usually be expected. Any updates that we know of for this guide will be on the Cicerone website (www.cicerone.co.uk/1003/updates), so please check before planning your trip. We also advise that you check information about such things as transport, accommodation and shops locally. Even rights of way can be altered over time.

We are always grateful for information about any discrepancies between a guidebook and the facts on the ground, sent by email to updates@cicerone.co.uk or by post to Cicerone, Juniper House, Murley Moss, Oxenholme Road, Kendal, LA9 7RL.

Register your book: To sign up to receive free updates, special offers and GPX files where available, register your book at www.cicerone.co.uk.

Front cover: The long whaleback ridge of Pendle Hill seen from Grindleton Fell (Walk 20)

WALKING IN LANCASHIRE

40 WALKS THROUGHOUT THE COUNTY INCLUDING THE FOREST OF BOWLAND AND RIBBLE VALLEY

by Mark Sutcliffe

JUNIPER HOUSE, MURLEY MOSS,
OXENHOLME ROAD, KENDAL, CUMBRIA LA9 7RL
www.cicerone.co.uk

Passing bluebell woods while heading up onto the fells near Grindleton (Walk 20)

CONTENTS

Route symbols on OS map extracts
(for OS legend see printed OS maps)

~ route

~ alternative route

(SF) start/finish point

(S) start point

(F) finish point

➤ route direction

SCALE: 1:50,000

0 kilometres 0.5 — 1
0 miles 0.5

Features on the overview map

National Park
eg **BRECON BEACONS**

Forest Park/National Forest
eg *National Forest*

Area of Outstanding Natural
Beauty/National Scenic Area
eg *Dedham Vale*

>800m
600m
400m
200m
75m
0m

GPX files for all routes can be downloaded free at www.cicerone.co.uk/1003/GPX.

Ottergear Bridge, conveying the Thirlmere Aqueduct across the River Conder (Walk 3)

Millpond calm at Grizedale Lea Reservoir (Walk 5)

INTRODUCTION

Pendle from the foothills above Downham (Walk 33)

From the wide-open expanses of Morecambe Bay to the limestone fringes of the Dales; from the rich industrial heritage of the West Pennine Moors to the wild vastness of the Forest of Bowland Area of Outstanding Natural Beauty (AONB), Lancashire offers some of the most varied walking anywhere in the UK.

Blessed with two Areas of Outstanding Natural Beauty, 160 kilometres of coastline, several chains of sparkling upland reservoirs, some internationally important nature reserves and two of England's largest river catchments, when it comes to natural assets, Lancashire is one of the wealthiest counties in all England.

With rolling foothills, verdant valleys and some of the most scenically stunning untamed landscapes in England, Lancashire has it all. Explore the gritstone moors, intimate valleys and bleak beauty of the lonely uplands of Lancashire, earning outstanding panoramic views from the summits of some surprisingly challenging hills in this varied selection of walks across the county.

Gragareth, the highest peak in Lancashire, is a proper mountain – just. Using the traditional mountain measure, at 627m high, Gragareth just sneaks over the bar and is eclipsed by the hulking 736m giant just a few kilometres to the east: Whernside (which is in Yorkshire).

On a clear day, Gragareth offers a pleasant and quite challenging walk worthy of a county high point. The views out over Morecambe Bay and the Cumbrian peninsulas are extensive, but offer a wistful reminder of what Lancashire lost several decades ago. Look carefully over the flanks of Barbon Low Fell from the summit plateau and the Old Man of Coniston looms tantalisingly on the horizon to the northwest. Until 1974, this iconic peak was once the highest mountain in the County Palatine of Lancashire.

In 1974, Merseyside, Cheshire and Greater Manchester swallowed up the urban fringes to the south of the county, while Lancashire annexed several bits of Yorkshire and vice versa. It was to the north that the Red Rose County suffered its most egregious losses. The area beyond the River Kent, including the low-lying fells of Furness and both Windermere and Coniston were all subsumed into Cumbria – a county forged from bits of Westmorland, Cumberland, the West Riding of Yorkshire and a large slice of Lancashire.

But make no mistake, the current borders of Lancashire still make it home to some very fine hills well worthy of walkers' attention: Pendle is a classic and the Bowland Fells provide a wonderful backdrop for a long weekend of exploration.

This carefully curated selection of walks offers something for everyone: from wild weekend adventures for committed hikers and challenging routes for seasoned walkers, to engaging urban hikes and shorter wildlife-rich walks for active families to enjoy.

This collection has been two years in the making. The first walks were undertaken just as the infamous 'Beast from the East' struck in the spring of 2018. Some of the early walks had to be abandoned as the snow lay in thick drifts on some of the scheduled routes.

Less than six months later, during the lengthy summer heatwave, I found myself exploring the parched uplands of the West Pennine Moors between Blackburn and Bolton. The very next day, these heather-clad slopes were consumed by wild fires as the tinder-dry peat went up in smoke. And that, in a nutshell, pretty much sums up the full spectrum of terrain and weather you can expect to encounter in Lancashire – sometimes all on the same day.

The beauty of this great county lies in the diversity of its landscapes, the warmth of its people and the depth of its history. From charming rambles along a canal-side towpath in the heart of a mill town into the countryside beyond, to challenging treks to the top of rugged mountains to earn outstanding views – the Red Rose County has it all.

The complex crinkles and creases of the Hareden Valley (Walk 6)

HISTORY

Some 50 years ago, Lancashire was significantly bigger than it was today and I could share an even greater range of walks than the compelling crop of routes collated here. Prior to the local government reorganisation of 1974, parts of what is now Cumbria (not to mention a few bits of Yorkshire) belonged to the Red Rose County.

In those days, the highest hill in Lancashire was the Old Man of Coniston – and a large swath of the southern Lake District fell within the county borders. This segment of the county – known as 'Lancashire over the Water' included much of the Furness Peninsula.

Go back even further, to the Middle Ages, and the County Palatine of Lancashire was an even larger entity which would today probably be

likened to a semi-autonomous region such Andalucía or Catalonia.

Edward III awarded this special status in 1351, in response to the House of Lancaster's strategic importance as a bulwark against marauding Scottish raiders. In those days the Duke of Lancaster enjoyed greater powers than the ruling classes of other counties and the Palatine covered much of the northwest of England, including what is now Merseyside and Greater Manchester.

Palatinate status became hereditary in 1362 upon the elevation of the most famous holder of the Dukedom: John of Gaunt, son of Edward III and de facto ruler during his father's illness. John of Gaunt's younger brother, Edmund, became Duke of York.

It was the ongoing dispute over the succession between John of

Gaunt's descendants and his younger brother Edmund's heirs that pitted the House of Lancaster against the House of York in a series of violent convulsions which shaped the monarchy for the next century and a half – known, of course, as The Wars of the Roses.

The intrigue and internecine skirmishing continued throughout the latter half of the 15th century, until opposition to the 'tyrant king' Richard III rallied around the House of Lancaster.

The Lancastrian Henry Tudor became the focus for the rebellion, returning from exile in France to defeat Richard at the battle of Bosworth in 1485. Henry married Elizabeth of York and thus united the two factions to rule as Henry VII. To symbolise the nation's new-found unity, Henry fused the Red Rose of Lancashire with the White Rose of Yorkshire to create the Tudor Rose – which remains a powerful emblem of England to this day.

The legacy of the Palatine's primacy persists today: the full text of the Loyal Toast salutes 'The Queen, Duke of Lancaster'. They are, in fact one and the same person, affirming the ties that bind the red rose of Lancashire to the red rose of England.

Another legacy that anyone visiting the further flung outposts of the county will quickly appreciate, is a profound sense of local pride and a fierce spirit of independence.

The mill towns of East Lancashire, Blackburn, Burnley, Nelson and Colne, were the crucibles for the noise and heat of the industrial revolution and the social and political upheavals that accompanied it.

As social reformers laboured to improve the lot of the millworkers, hard-won rights, such as shorter working hours and even the occasional paid holiday, provided the emergent urban working class with recreational opportunities.

Many spent their free time in the inns and taverns that occupied every corner of the mill towns, but others sought solace and sanctuary by exploring the moors of the West Pennines – bringing them into direct conflict with local landowners. The seeds for the set-piece confrontations of the 1930s on Kinder Scout were actually sown on the moors above Blackburn and Darwen nearly 50 years earlier.

And yet in the north of the county – particularly in the Forest of Bowland – the landscapes have scarcely changed for centuries. This is a side of Lancashire which few people outside the county fully appreciate: that beyond the industry and the urban sprawl lie thousands of square kilometres of largely undiscovered country.

LANDSCAPE AND GEOLOGY

The West Pennine Hills and the uplands that stretch from the Bowland Fells to the Ribble Valley and from the Lune to the Calder largely comprise millstone grit – a type of sandstone

Lonely barn on the fellside below Bowland Knotts (Walk 4)

which, as its name suggests, was tough enough to be used to mill flour and the oats that fared better in the north.

Out to the west, the fertile flat-lands of the Fylde and the West Lancashire Plain are largely silt which more closely resemble the Fens, but in the north-eastern corner of the county, where the sandstone meets the lime-stone, the geology is more complex, with the occasional limestone outcrop erupting through the gritstone.

In the south of the county, the mill towns sprawl along the valley floors, but the sunlit uplands of the West Pennines are only a short, sharp climb away. The gradients can be punishing – especially in the steep-sided valleys

(or 'cloughs') eroded by the swift flowing stream and rivers draining the uplands. To some, these moorlands are a bit bleak, but for anyone with an interest in industrial archaeology, the legacy of the mills and mining herea-bouts provide a number of rich seams to explore.

To the north, the quality of the views increases in direct proportion to the altitude. Iconic Pendle Hill, which can be seen from most of Lancashire's principal towns and cities, can claim summit views to Snowdon, Scafell Pike and The Roaches in Staffordshire.

But actually, the best views lie fur-ther west, on the edge of the Pennines and the fringe of the Bowland Fells, where the vistas can also encompass

The causeway to Sunderland Point (Walk 18)

more comprehensive views of the Lakeland fells, the Isle of Man and – very occasionally – the Mountains of Mourne in Northern Ireland.

WILDLIFE

Lancashire is something of a bird-watchers' paradise, offering some notable coastal birding and more than its fair share of nature reserves. The Lancashire Wildlife Trust covers what could perhaps be loosely regarded as 'Greater Lancashire' comprising Manchester and Liverpool and controls a number of excellent reserves including the innovative Brockholes Nature Reserve just off the M6 near Preston.

The RSPB reserve at Leighton Moss (see Walk 19) is home to rarities like the bittern and the bearded tit, while the Wildlife and Wetlands Trust's Martin Mere hosts some amazing waders and wildfowl.

The peaty uplands of Bowland and the West Pennines are home to some highly specialist plants and animals. The peat itself is increasingly valued as an enormously efficient carbon sink – locking up many times more carbon than woodlands. In late spring, the peat is dotted with the fluffy white seed heads of cotton grass, while the limestone outcrops of East Lancashire are home to some elusive orchids. The verdant meadows of Bowland are studded with an array of wildflowers from May to July, and the heather of the West Pennines is punctuated with dense stands of bilberry (a relative of the blueberry) and which makes the most sublime of crumbles.

Bilberries ripening on top of Grindleton Fell (Walk 20)

Red squirrels can still be found among the native woodlands of North and West Lancashire and the Forest of Bowland is home to several species of deer which roam wild across the landscape.

Perhaps the most iconic species is also to be found among the remote valleys and fells of Bowland – the hen harrier. Numbers plummeted a few years ago and there were concerns that this elegant bird of prey would be lost in what was one of its last strongholds, but the Bowland population is recovering and the chances of seeing this glorious raptor 'sky dancing' over the uplands in spring are now better than they have been for a decade or so.

HOW TO GET THERE

Lancashire is well served by motorways (M6, M62, M61, M65) and mainline rail, with major transport interchanges at Preston, Blackburn, Bury and Lancaster. Avanti West Coast, Northern Rail or Virgin Transpennine Express operate the majority of services serving the county. Preston is a little over two hours away by train from London, an hour from Manchester and just over an hour from Leeds

15

Slaidburn, in the Forest of Bowland (Walk 21)

with regular onward connections to Blackburn, Burnley and Clitheroe.

GETTING AROUND

Most of the county's cities and major towns are served by rail links and the bus services are, on the whole, reasonably reliable. The overwhelmingly rural Forest of Bowland AONB is more difficult to reach by public transport, although the Bentham line running from Settle to Morecambe links up several towns and villages on the northern edge of the AONB.

BASES

Most of the major towns and cities have a comprehensive choice of accommodation, with the leafier outlying suburbs of Preston, Chorley, Blackburn and Burnley offering a good range of B&Bs and small hotels. As a popular tourist destination, Lancaster also has an excellent choice of city centre accommodation, with good links to the northern fringe of the Forest of Bowland.

The smaller towns and villages of East Lancashire – lying in the shadow of Pendle – provide good access to attractive walking country, and the Ribble Valley, with its principal town of Clitheroe, also makes a good central base. In the Forest of Bowland, Slaidburn is the principal centre of population, but accommodation here is quite limited.

FOOD AND DRINK

Lancashire is increasingly acknowledged as one of the UK's leading foodie destinations – a reputation based on a growing number of Michelin-starred restaurants, who rely on the growing community of artisan food producers operating in the rural hinterland. Food markets and specialist independent retailers have prospered in recent years – although the locals will tell you they never went away.

Beyond the high-profile Michelin-starred establishments such as Northcote, the White Swan or Moor Hall, you'll find a selection of gastropubs in the towns and villages of the Ribble Valley and Forest of Bowland. Standout examples include Freemasons at Wiswell, the Parker's Arms in Newton, the iconic Inn at Whitewell and even out of the way, rural B&Bs like Dale House Barn near Slaidburn. Most of these establishments welcome walkers and some are even dog-friendly.

They take beer very seriously in this part of the world and the area is blessed with some fantastic village pubs and independent breweries. Thwaites, who first started brewing Wainwright (the well-known walkers' post-walk tipple) in tribute to the eponymous fell walker and guidebook author, still manages a number of popular walkers' watering holes in the county, while Moorhouses of Burnley will always be associated with Pendle Hill. Also worth seeking out are the cask offerings from Bowland Brewery in Clitheroe, Farm Yard Ales in Lancaster and Northern Whisper Brewing Co. in the Rossendale Valley.

WHEN TO GO

Lancashire is not noted for its balmy, benign climate. The textiles industry gravitated to the valleys of East Lancashire because the perennial damp prevented the cotton fibres from breaking on the looms and one of the reasons for the richness of the landscape in Lancashire is the climate, which is dominated by rainfall…lots of it! Weather systems come sweeping in off the Irish Sea and are funnelled up into the hills, where the clouds tend to shed their load with predictable regularity.

Snow is increasingly rare – although the uplands of Bowland regularly receive a frosting of snow and ice, and winter conditions up there need to be treated with respect.

Despite this, Lancashire is a year-round destination and some of these walks – especially Pendle and Great Hill – are best undertaken on a cold, crisp, mid-winter morning, when the views will be simply sensational.

Unlike Britain's southern counties, where winter suddenly gives way to summer sometime around the end of April, spring remains a delight in Lancashire, unfolding slowly in the valley bottoms initially and then ascending the slopes to the higher ground. It will often be wet and boggy underfoot, but the daffodils, primroses and bluebells provide a riot of colour from the end of February through to mid May when the fields resonate with enthusiastic bleating of new-born lambs.

Late spring and summer bring an influx of migrants to the uplands – including ring ouzel, curlew, whimbrel and hen harriers, who take to the skies above the Bowland Fells to perform their spectacular 'sky dance' courtship displays.

May and June are arguably the best months to visit – when the wildflowers are at their best and the Pennine colour palette at its most vibrant.

Autumn comes early to the uplands, with the heather turning auburn in tandem with the woodland canopy. This is a time of plenty across the pastureland, when the farming communities come together to celebrate the harvest at a string of rural shows and festivals as a pleasant precursor to the harsher days of winter.

ACCESS LAND

The upland moors of Lancashire were among some of the first areas of Britain to be opened up to public access under the Countryside and Rights of Way Act in 2000. Technically, this grants the public the right to roam over vast tracts of the county, but in practice some restrictions do exist. Consult the guidelines posted at popular access points, take an OS map (see below for the relevant sheets), and you can lose yourself in thousands of acres of deserted moorland, although do bear in mind that navigating across pathless terrain can be quite challenging – especially in adverse weather conditions. Find out more at www.naturalengland.co.uk or search for Natural England at www.gov.uk.

FOOTPATHS

Footpath maintenance is an area that has been neglected by some local authorities owing to austerity and budget cuts and, as a consequence, the quality of stiles, gates and signage varies quite widely across the

Looking west across the moorland from Bowland Knotts (Walk 4)

Mere Sands Wood Nature Reserve (Walk 26)

county. In the course of researching this guide, some of the urban local authorities would appear to be taking their responsibilities to maintain access more seriously than their rural counterparts. In particular, Pendle, Blackburn and Wyre councils continue to do an excellent job of promoting and protecting access to footpaths. This is not always the case in some of the more rural areas and some footpaths and access points have deteriorated noticeably in recent years. Where I have encountered problems, these have been logged with Lancashire County Council's Rights of Way Team (prow@lancashire.gov.uk; tel 01772 530317) and the relevant local authority.

SAFETY

The Pennines and Bowland Fells offer safe walking year round, but these exposed upland environments should be treated with respect at all times. Bowland Pennine Mountain Rescue and Rossendale and Pendle Mountain Rescue annually experience more than 100 callouts across the county and provide an essential service to the thousands of walkers who visit the county's hills throughout the year.

Conditions on the hills – particularly in winter – can rapidly deteriorate and a slip or a fall resulting in a broken or sprained ankle can suddenly turn a pleasant walk into a potentially risky situation – especially if nightfall is approaching.

Mobile phones

While mobile phones are becoming increasingly popular as navigation devices, they should not be your sole means of navigation. Locking onto a GPS signal depletes the battery more rapidly and may leave you in a vulnerable situation if you need to use the phone in an emergency.

The signal in the wilder reaches of Bowland is patchy and unreliable, so the basic safety and survival information provided above could be critical in an emergency. Take a paper map, plot your route in advance and tell someone where you're headed and when you'll be back.

BEFORE SETTING OUT

Plan your route and commit it to paper. If you are staying at a hotel or B&B, tell your hosts where you plan to go and give an estimated time of return.

Check the forecast and adjust your plans accordingly if extreme weather – especially snow and ice – is predicted.

Have a realistic understanding of your abilities and remain within them. Some of the walks in this guide cover more than 20 kilometres with several hundred metres of ascent. These will take at least six hours to complete, so set off early and allocate a realistic amount of time for rest stops and breaks – especially in winter.

The River Wyre with the Bowland Fells beyond (Walk 25)

WHAT TO TAKE

Essential:
- Map (and the ability to read it)
- Compass
- Torch (with spare batteries)
- Walking boots
- Waterproofs
- Gloves and hat
- Spare clothing
- High-energy snacks
- Water
- Whistle

Good to have:
- Survival bag
- Hot drinks
- First-aid kit
- Portable battery booster (to recharge your mobile phone)

IN AN EMERGENCY

If you do get into difficulties and need assistance, dial 999 and ask for Police and Mountain Rescue. If you have a casualty in your group, at least one person must stay with them. Do not leave the casualty alone while you seek help. When requesting help, provide as accurate a description of your location as possible. A grid reference will allow the rescue team to devise a rescue plan and provide assistance much more quickly.

It may seem dramatic, but given the remoteness and terrain of the Bowland Fells and West Pennine Moors, the local Air Ambulance may offer the best means of rescue. This service is funded entirely by charitable donations, so you may wish to consider supporting this life-saving service: nwaa.net.

MAPS

The maps you'll need to explore Lancashire are:

- OS Outdoor Leisure 1:25 000
- OL 21 South Pennines

The shooter's track leading back down to the Upper Wyre valley (Walk 10)

- OL 41 Forest of Bowland & Ribblesdale
- OS Explorer Series 1:25 000
- 285 Southport & Chorley
- 286 Blackpool & Preston
- 287 West Pennine Moors
- 296 Lancaster, Morecambe & Fleetwood

USING THIS GUIDE

Many walking books make a beeline for the walking 'honeypots' in North and East Lancashire, of which there are many. However, in researching this edition, I have tried to include walks in some of the less obvious, but more accessible, areas in the south and west of the county and, in so doing, offer a flavour of the rich industrial and cultural heritage of Lancashire as well as its diverse natural history.

In the more remote areas, I have tried to offer up longer, more challenging routes that justify quite a lengthy drive, but I have also tried to include shorter walks on the urban fringe of the more populated areas for those who enjoy an afternoon or evening walk after work.

With the exception of the walk over Whalley Nab and the spectacular Bowland Traverse – a two-day linear trek across the wonderfully wild Forest of Bowland AONB – all the walks are circular. To cater for all tastes and to ensure a little variety, I've included a couple of urban routes too.

GPX tracks

GPX tracks for the routes in this guidebook are available to download free at www.cicerone.co.uk/1003/GPX. GPX files are provided in good faith, but neither the author nor the publisher accept responsibility for their accuracy.

NORTH LANCASHIRE AND
THE BOWLAND FELLS

The view southwest to Pendle from above Stocks Reservoir (Walk 9)

WALK 1

Beacon Fell and Brock Valley

Start/finish	Car park at Brock Bottom, Claughton (SD 549 431)
Distance	8km (5 miles)
Total ascent	220m
Time	3hr
Map	OS Explorer OL41
Refreshments	Beacon Fell Visitor Centre

This pretty route combines a riverside woodland walk through an intimate valley with a steady climb to the modest 266m summit of Beacon Fell, which punches well above its weight when it comes to expansive views.

From the car park, head upstream past the picnic tables and cross the bridge then turn left over the cattle grid and left again past **Brockmill** and over a stile into the meadow.

Follow the path across the fields, with the river away to the left. After 400 metres, at the corner of field, head left over the stile to join the riverside path. Continue upstream, following the river as it meanders round right and the path climbs through the woods of the Brock Valley to a track. Head left along the track then skirt right of the house and continue along the edge of the woods.

After 500 metres, beside the footbridge, follow a rocky track round to the right then follow the lane for 250 metres, taking the footpath on the left where the lane curves right. Descend through trees and where the track heads left, continue ahead over the footbridge and past the campfire pit onto the gravel track through the Scout camp (**Activity Centre** on the map) to rejoin the river.

Follow the riverside footpath for 400 metres, then go over a stile into open meadow. Continue across the fields

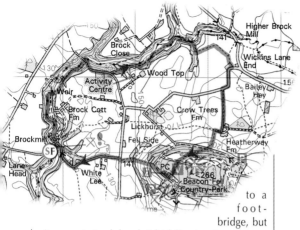

to a foot-bridge, but don't cross. Instead, head right following the tributary over a stile and into woods. Cross the feeder stream at the next footbridge and turn left to climb through trees to cross a stile onto open farmland.

Straight ahead, the views east to the Bleasdale fells open up. Follow a grassy path along the left-hand edge of field then through a gateway and half right along the edge of the next field. Then follow signs directing you right over a series of stiles to join a lane.

Follow the lane right for 300 metres, taking the track on the left to continue over fields towards the wooded escarpment of Beacon Fell. Continue to the residential hamlet at **Heatherway Farm**; go right over the stile next to a pond, then left alongside marker posts and over another stile to the perimeter road of **Beacon Fell Country Park**.

As its name suggests, **Beacon Fell** was one of a chain of beacons which spanned the nation to warn of invasion during the Spanish and Napoleonic Wars. More recently, in 1970, it became one of Britain's first designated Country Parks.

Cross the road and climb diagonally right through the pines and straight ahead over the heath to the **Visitor**

25

The Bleasdale fells from the slopes of Beacon Fell

The views west over Morecambe Bay are best from the edge of the clear-felled heath above the Visitor Centre.

Centre. The summit viewpoint is well worth a short detour for panoramic views over the Ribble Valley and Forest of Bowland. ◀

From the Visitor Centre, head right along the perimeter lane for 250 metres and take the footpath on the left. Look straight out west over Morecambe Bay from the top of this path on a clear day and you might be able to make out the Isle of Man, almost 100 kilometres away in the distance.

Descending steeply through woods and fields, go right at the lane, then left along White Lee Lane for 800 metres back to the car park.

WALK 2
Bleasdale Ridge circular

Start/finish	Delph Lane car park, Oakenclough (SD 546 455)
Distance	15.5km (9¾ miles)
Total ascent	458m
Time	5hr
Map	OS Explorer OL41
Refreshments	Beacon Fell Country Park, Chipping Farm Shop

This rewarding walk follows the natural contours of the landscape to complete the northern rim of the Bleasdale Horseshoe before descending the steep nose of Fair Snape and meandering through the rich pastureland beneath the fells via a mysterious prehistoric henge. In the right conditions, the panoramic views from this western rampart of the Bowland Fells are simply stunning.

Park at Delph Lane car park and walk north up the lane past Tramper Trail to turn right along the track beyond the cottage at Stang Yule. Fork left then back right through a kissing gate onto access land. Continue northeast along the edge of a felled plantation.

Climbing onto **Oakenclough Fell**, the views behind you over the Fylde plain, Lune estuary, Morecambe Bay and the Irish Sea open out magnificently. Continue northeast alongside the wall, then follow the track up onto **Hazelhurst Fell**.

Just below the trig point (hidden from view above the skyline northwest) on Hazelhurst Fell, follow the track as it descends before climbing again up to Fiendsdale Head. At a junction of tracks, head left, climbing towards Fiendsdale Head.

A modest **memorial** beside the track commemorates the RAF personnel who lost their lives in military aircraft which crashed among these hills in adverse weather conditions during and after World War 2.

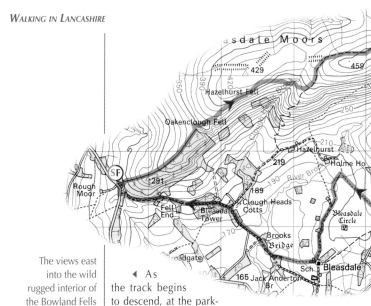

The views east into the wild rugged interior of the Bowland Fells are magnificent, as Ingleborough looms above the craggy outcrops of Bowland Knotts.

◀ As the track begins to descend, at the parking place, take the faint path off right to follow the white marker posts east across the heather to Fiendsdale Head.

When the marker posts run out, make for the wire fence and pick up the flagged path at the kissing gate. Follow the flags east for 100 metres then continue

Memorial to members of RAF air crews lost among the Bowland Fells

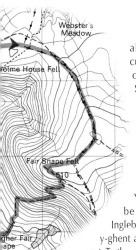

alongside the wire fence as it curves gently round to the south onto the summit plateau of **Fair Snape Fell**.

This stretch can be hard going as the peat hags are quite badly eroded in places. Hopping over to the other side of the fence can make things a little easier.

Your endeavours will be rewarded by **views** of Ingleborough's companions, Pen-y-ghent and Whernside away to the east. To the north, the Lakeland fells form a dramatic backdrop to Morecambe Bay. On a clear day, you may catch a glimpse of the Isle of Man away to the northwest.

To the southwest, the foothills of Snowdonia are clearly visible and, in exceptional atmospheric conditions, the highest summits in the Mountains of Mourne in Northern Ireland are just visible on the horizon.

Continue through the kissing gate and follow the path round to the southwest to the summit cairn. From the cairn, head southeast along the ridge towards Parlick before cutting back on a steep zigzag track down the western face of Fair Snape Fell.

At the access point, follow the faint path across the field to **Higher Fair Snape Farm**. Go through the farmyard then left and right at the signpost on the track to the right of another barn. At end of the track to **Holme House**, go left down the track to Vicarage Farm.

At the farm, a concessionary footpath takes you to **Bleasdale Circle**. ▸

It's unclear exactly who built **Bleasdale Circle**, but it could date back to the Neolithic Period. There's

It doesn't rival Stonehenge but it's an atmospheric spot in a little coppice atop a shallow hillock beneath the Bleasdale fells.

The Bleasdale Fells form a stunning backdrop to the Neolithic Bleasdale Circle

little to see on the ground, but interpretation boards explain how the site may have looked more than 5000 years ago. There is evidence that a high-status individual was buried here and, even today, it remains an inexplicably evocative place.

After returning to the track, continue south to the **church** then take the footpath right across fields to the lane and past the old packhorse **Bridge** at Brooks. Continue along the lane past **Bleasdale Tower** and **Fell End**, then cut across on a footpath running south of Stang Yule back to Delph Lane.

WALK 3
Clougha Pike

Start/finish	Rigg Lane car park, Quernmore (SD 526 604)
Distance	11.5km (7 miles)
Total ascent	430m
Time	4hr
Map	OS Explorer OL41
Refreshments	Station Inn, Caton

This shortish scramble over the gnarly clitter and spoil heaps of Clougha Pike is a rite of passage for all outdoorsy types from the historic city of Lancaster. The ascent is steep in places, but rewarded with excellent views from the summit out over Morecambe Bay.

Leave the car park via the footpath, climbing through the bracken and keeping right on the rocky track then across the bog on a wooden walkway. Continue climbing through the scrub and into the woodland beside a stream.

At the wall, take the right-hand ladder stile and continue climbing alongside the wall. ▶ As the gradient plateaus, head half right for the corner of wall ahead, then follow the wall through the wooden gate.

This path can be become a stream in wet weather.

Ascend diagonally southeast up the ridge via the rocky scarp of **Clougha Scar** then follow the wall right towards the summit. After 800 metres, go left through the kissing gate and over the stile, then follow a wire fence and head up over slabs to the cairn and onwards to the trig adorning the summit of **Clougha Pike**.

Leave the trig point and head just north of east on the rocky path towards Grit Fell, crossing the wire fence and descending through the heather before climbing again towards Grit Fell.

After another 800 metres, cross another wire fence and follow the tumble-down wall to go over the lad-der stile to the summit of **Grit Fell** – marked by a modest cairn. Continue along the rocky path, heading east towards Ward's Stone and, after 800 metres, take the shooters' track hard left.

Look out for the prominent sculptures to the left of the track, then continue along the track to the prominent stone outcrop on the left at SD 552 596 and take the faint footpath descending right through the heather.

Andy Goldsworthy's imposing sculptures above the quarry workings on Clougha

Gerald, the late sixth Duke of Westminster and owner of the Abbeystead Estate, commissioned art-ist Andy Goldsworthy to create these **monolithic installations** over three consecutive years strad-dling the millennium. Some people refer to them

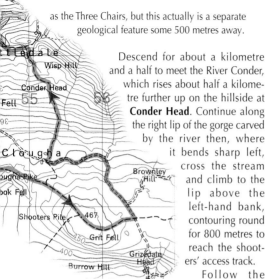

as the Three Chairs, but this actually is a separate geological feature some 500 metres away.

Descend for about a kilometre and a half to meet the River Conder, which rises about half a kilometre further up on the hillside at **Conder Head**. Continue along the right lip of the gorge carved by the river then, where it bends sharp left, cross the stream and climb to the lip above the left-hand bank, contouring round for 800 metres to reach the shooters' access track.

Follow the track downhill for 500 metres and before the gate at the edge of the access land, take the grassy trod off left which leads to the rather striking Ottergear Bridge, carrying the pipeline from Thirlmere to Manchester.

The **Thirlmere Aqueduct** is the longest gravity-fed aqueduct in Britain, carrying water almost 160 kilometres from the Lake District to Manchester. Built between 1890 and 1925, it is capable of transporting 227 million litres of water every day – that's roughly 100 Olympic swimming pools' worth of water. Water flows at around six and a half kilometres an hour, taking just over a day to complete the journey.

Cross the bridge and continue along the grassy path past the large stone block and back to the car park near **Quernmore**.

WALK 4
Cross of Greet and Bowland Knotts

Start/finish	Cross of Greet Bridge car park (SD 703 590)
Distance	12km (7½ miles)
Total ascent	430m
Time	4hr
Map	OS Explorer OL41
Refreshments	Hark to Bounty, Slaidburn
Public transport	Dales Bus 881 and 833 Bowland Explorer (summer Sundays only)

This satisfying hike connects the highpoints of the two single track passes which traverse the Forest of Bowland from north to south. Bowland Knotts is a gnarly natural rocky outcrop offering expansive views, while the Cross of Greet refers to the site of a medieval stone cross which stood at the head of the pass.

Follow the faint path east across boggy tussock grass above the infant **River Hodder**. Go through sheepfolds and cross the Kearsden Brook to reach a track then footpath on the left that climbs northeast past farm buildings at **Catlow** and a lonely barn on the fellside.

As the gradient levels off, take a sharp left turn through a gate where the dry stone walls meet, then follow a rough track northeast towards the craggy outcrops of **Bowland Knotts**.

Join the road and climb briefly north over the cattle grid then turn 90 degrees left at the rough parking area, following the rocky ridge southwest towards the trig point on the most prominent outcrop.

This is access land and a network of faint paths traverse these weathered gritstone crags before coalescing into a more distinct path running northwest then west alongside the wall.

Continue west, descending first, then climbing past the remote outcrops of **Cold Stone** and Ravens Castle to the intersection of the dry stone wall and a wire fence. Head left along the wire fence descending steadily over boggy peat hags to reach the road at **Cross of Greet**.

The quiet road leading up to Cross of Greet

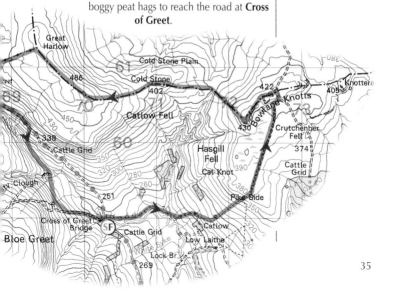

The rusting hulk of the steam crane in the quarry below Cross of Greet

The **Cross of Greet** was a large sandstone cross which once marked the boundary between Lancashire and Yorkshire. While the cross is long gone, the base stone – with an obvious hole into which the cross would have slotted – can still be seen to the north of the cattle grid.

Descend southeast down the road for 800 metres, then follow one of the faint paths down to the stream and ford with care. Continue along the far bank, climbing to the well-hidden abandoned **quarry** at SD 694 596. After exploring, continue southeast to pick up a shooters' track that returns to **Cross of Greet Bridge**.

It's hard to imagine that this remote, tranquil valley would once have echoed to the clank of quarrying and the clatter of wagons rattling down the railway to the massive dam construction site about three kilometres away at Stocks Reservoir. However, you can still find the remains of a **steam-powered crane and narrow-gauge railway** in the secluded quarry just a short walk from the car park at the Cross of Greet Bridge.

WALK 5

Grizedale and Nicky Nook

Start/finish	Scorton village centre (SD 502 486)
Distance	8.5km (5¼ miles)
Total ascent	220m
Time	2hr 30min
Map	OS Explorer OL41
Refreshments	The Barn, Scorton; The Apple Store, Wyresdale Park
Public transport	512 from Garstang

This walk offers a variety of scenery, from fells to woodland to water, and has some great views from above Grizedale Lea and Barnacre Reservoirs on a clear day. Scorton is a picturesque village with a number of places to eat.

Starting from the centre of Scorton, turn right in front of the Priory and go up Snowhill Lane and over the M6. Follow signs for **Wyresdale Park** and the Apple Store café. Continue along the track past the house and the café to a cattle grid then along the lake shore to a wooden gate. Go right here, following the track for 500 metres past farm buildings and a little copse to join the road. Follow the road east for 300 metres, then turn right onto a lane and follow it through a metal gate as it becomes a track into woodland. After a second metal gate, bear right towards the bridge.

The short climb to the trig point and summit of **Nicky Nook** is recommended on a clear day – the views are well worth it.

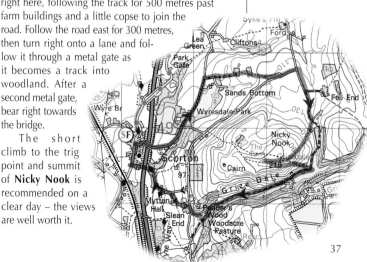

37

The 215m summit of **Nicky Nook**, although modest in height, offers splendid views over Lancashire's coastal plain, Morecambe Bay and beyond to the Lakeland fells. On a really clear day it is possible to see the Isle of Man and the Great Orme on the North Wales coast. Birds such as meadow pipits and skylarks are common on the fell, while the more fortunate may catch a glimpse of tree pipits or yellowhammers.

The reservoirs above Grizedale, Grizedale Lea and Barnacre, attract several hundred rare whimbrel, which fly in to roost at the site during their migration from Africa to Iceland in April and May.

After admiring the view, drop back down on the steep stepped path descending southeast to the **Grizedale Reservoir**. Join the waterside path heading right; keep following the track along the Grizedale Valley for almost a kilometre and a half. ◀ At the metal gate, head right onto the footpath signed Higher Lane and continue to the top of the hill and through the gate at the top.

Head right and follow the road for 50 metres to take the public footpath waymarker on the left and follow the left boundary of the field before heading diagonally right towards the bottom of the field.

Cross the wooden stile and continue straight across the next field to join the road. Turn left onto the road and continue straight on and underneath the motorway. At the T-junction, go right into the village of Scorton.

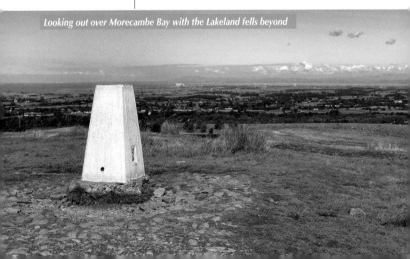

Looking out over Morecambe Bay with the Lakeland fells beyond

WALK 6
Langden and Hareden Valleys

Start/finish	Langden lay-by beside Trough of Bowland road (SD 633 511)
Distance	10km (6¼ miles)
Total ascent	320m
Time	3hr
Map	OS Explorer OL41
Refreshments	Puddleducks, Dunsop Bridge

This is a classic walk which showcases the best of Bowland's secluded valleys and wild uplands. It can be hard going in places, with rivers to ford and boggy ground to negotiate, but on a dry day in late spring, it's one of the best walks in Bowland.

Follow the tarmac avenue to the **Water Works** buildings and continue past Langden intake, following the track southwest beside the **Langden Brook**. After 800 metres or so, follow the track as it climbs away from the river and continue for 200 metres, taking the left-hand fork where the track levels out.

> In April and May, look out for **ring ouzels** in the hawthorn trees on the far side of Langden Valley. These rare blackbirds with a distinctive white bib are spring migrants which only nest in a handful of places in the north of England.

After just over three kilometres, the track descends to **Langden Castle**, which is actually a barn with some rather ornate, arched windows and door. At the front of the 'castle', locate a faint path through the rushes heading south up the Bleadale Valley.

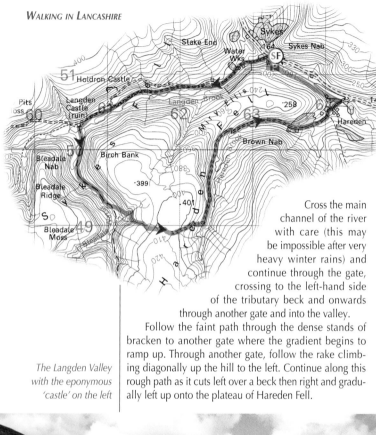

Cross the main channel of the river with care (this may be impossible after very heavy winter rains) and continue through the gate, crossing to the left-hand side of the tributary beck and onwards through another gate and into the valley.

Follow the faint path through the dense stands of bracken to another gate where the gradient begins to ramp up. Through another gate, follow the rake climbing diagonally up the hill to the left. Continue along this rough path as it cuts left over a beck then right and gradually left up onto the plateau of Hareden Fell.

The Langden Valley with the eponymous 'castle' on the left

Here, the path peters out, but head for the first white marker post. Don't be tempted to follow the line of posts. Instead, head half left, picking your way across the peat hags heading just south of east for 500 metres.

At the summit of **Hareden Fell**, the views open out across the bleak moorlands of Bowland: the verdant beauty of the valleys obscured by the lie of the land – accentuating the loneliness of this last bastion of English wilderness. It's right up there with the likes of the North Pennines, Dartmoor and the Cheviots.

Head for a modest marker stone jutting like jaws out of the peat. Grouse butts appear ahead and head for the parking space at the top of a shooters' track descending north into the **Hareden Valley**. Continue along this track for about one and a half kilometres, crossing a footbridge, passing another water intake and onto a tarmac drive alongside woodland.

Follow the track between the farmhouses and over a stream, then 150 metres before its junction with the Trough road, go left through a gate and diagonally across a paddock to a stile next to the brook. Continue upstream beside the brook, crossing a stile on your left and into a field to return over another bridge to the lay-by at **Langden**.

Looking south up Bleadale Beck to the fells above

41

WALK 7
Parlick Pike and Fair Snape

Start/finish	Parking spaces below Fell Foot Farm, near Chipping (SD 602 442)
Distance	9.5km (6 miles)
Total ascent	420m
Time	3hr
Map	OS Explorer OL41
Refreshments	Cobbled Corner Café, Chipping

A classic, short hill walk that's equally rewarding as a summer evening sprint or a half-day hike on a crisp winter's day. The steep initial ascent gets you up high rapidly for amazing views out over Morecambe Bay.

Go through the gate and after 100 metres take the left-hand fork, unless you want to tackle the seriously steep direct route up to Parlick summit.

Climb steadily northwest as the views extend out over Beacon Fell to the Fylde plain. At the gate, stop to admire the views over to Blackpool Tower (you can almost hear the screams of delight from the pleasure beach) then head

The edge of Blindhurst Fell curves away to Fair Snape

right (north-east) along-side the fence and ascend to the summit of **Parlick**.

At the rather ramshackle cairn, cross the stile and keep left of the fence into a shallow depression before climbing steadily along the edge of **Blindhurst Fell** towards the sum-mit of Fair Snape. Follow the wall almost to the pla-teau edge then strike out half left, following the path through a kissing gate to **Fair Snape Fell** summit cairn.

The **views** that open from up here can be little short of astounding. On a calm, clear, early summer's evening, which sometimes produces an atmos-pheric lensing effect, the horizon comes almost close enough to touch.

You might make out the Isle of Man or even the Mountains of Mourne in Northern Ireland. To the north, Morecambe Bay and the Lakeland fells loom large, while to the east, the Yorkshire Three Peaks dominate the skyline and to the southwest, across Liverpool Bay, the mountains of Snowdonia are usually visible.

From the summit shelter, follow the faint path east to meet the junction of two wire fences. Cross the stile to the eastern side of the fence running north and follow it for 400 metres to meet a track.

Pendle Hill and Birdie Brow from Saddle Fell

Follow the track just south of east as the views open up over the whaleback ridge of Pendle and beyond to the West Pennine Moors. Through the kissing gate, follow the path right downhill for just over a kilometre to the gate at the edge of access land. Follow the muddy/grassy track downhill to **Saddle End Farm**.

Continue down through farmyard then turn back on yourself to take the footpath over a stile on the right. Continue west on the footpath over the somewhat marshy pastures and over the beck to **Wolfen Hall**.

Beyond the farm, cross the farm track and follow the footpath across the fields on the edge of access land to the start point at the foot of Parlick.

WALK 8
Roeburndale – the enchanted valley

Start/finish	Car park at Bridge House Garden Centre, Wray (SD 606 675)
Distance	11.5km (7¼ miles)
Total ascent	360m
Time	3hr 30min
Map	OS Explorer OL41
Refreshments	Bridge House Tearooms
Public transport	80, 81 Lancaster to Ingleton

Roeburndale is one of the most enchanting valleys in the whole of Bowland – a steep-sided gorge densely wooded with native broadleaf trees forming an almost subtropical microclimate where rare species still flourish.

Leave Bridge House Farm tearooms and continue straight ahead up the steep lane of Helks Brow for just under one kilometre, passing on your left the sawmill at **Above Beck**. Take the footpath on the right to cross the river via the footbridge, then climb up the other side to **Alcocks Farm**.

At Alcocks Farm, follow the lane uphill for 500 metres, then cross the stone stile on the right and head half left to a narrow squeeze stile. Continue climbing along right field boundary towards a barn on the skyline. Pass to the right of the barn, crossing the wooden stile in the corner of the field.

Continue along the hedge line, crossing the farm track leading to **Outhwaite**, and alongside a dry stone wall, before moving onto a grassy field track, passing through two gates and descending gently to cross the beck and go through another gate. The track becomes less obvious, but continue more or less straight on, past a wooden marker post and over a stone stile. Follow the

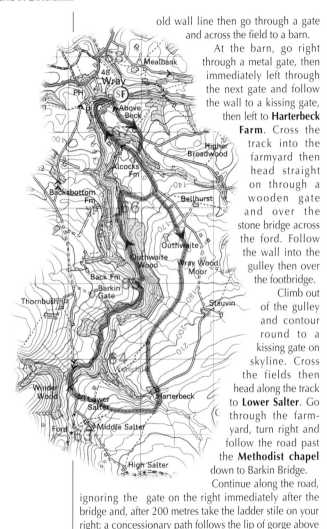

old wall line then go through a gate and across the field to a barn.

At the barn, go right through a metal gate, then immediately left through the next gate and follow the wall to a kissing gate, then left to **Harterbeck Farm**. Cross the track into the farmyard then head straight on through a wooden gate and over the stone bridge across the ford. Follow the wall into the gulley then over the footbridge.

Climb out of the gulley and contour round to a kissing gate on skyline. Cross the fields then head along the track to **Lower Salter**. Go through the farmyard, turn right and follow the road past the **Methodist chapel** down to Barkin Bridge.

Continue along the road, ignoring the gate on the right immediately after the bridge and, after 200 metres take the ladder stile on your right; a concessionary path follows the lip of gorge above the woods then descends into Roeburndale and a footbridge over the river.

In August 1967, Roeburndale was devastated by
The Great Flood, which was triggered by a summer
cloudburst. A wall of water demolished 13 houses,
cottages and barns, deposited 24-tonne rocks 400
metres down-river, took out every bridge in the valley and killed dozens of livestock.

Remain on the west bank and, after a kilometre,
cross the **River Roeburn** at the footbridge and follow it
along the east bank for another kilometre and across an
open field to a substantial footbridge. Do not cross the
bridge, but continue to far side of field and follow the
path climbing half left up through woods and over the
fields to rejoin the road. Turn left and follow the road for
two kilometres back into **Wray village**.

*The entire Roeburn
Valley is densely
wooded*

WALK 9
Stocks Reservoir circular

Start/finish	School Lane car park, Dalehead, near Slaidburn (SD 546 455)
Distance	11km (6¾ miles)
Total ascent	240m
Time	3hr 30min
Map	OS Explorer OL41
Refreshments	Fishing lodge at Stocks Reservoir

In the rolling hills above Slaidburn, at the heart of the Forest of Bowland, lies Stocks Reservoir – a tranquil oasis and haven for wildlife that feels more like a Scottish loch than something confected by the water board in a quiet corner of Lancashire.

From the car park, go through the kissing gate and follow the path right (north) (past the picnic area and bird hides on the left), and into woodland to emerge in open farmland, climbing steadily away from the head of **Stocks Reservoir**.

The rolling hills above Stocks Reservoir from the eastern shore

Stocks Reservoir was opened by HRH Prince George on 5 July 1932 and supplies the Fylde coast

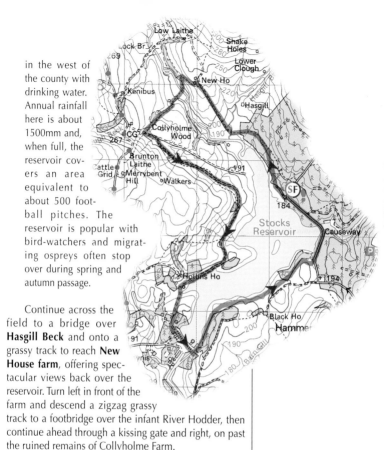

in the west of the county with drinking water. Annual rainfall here is about 1500mm and, when full, the reservoir covers an area equivalent to about 500 football pitches. The reservoir is popular with bird-watchers and migrating ospreys often stop over during spring and autumn passage.

Continue across the field to a bridge over **Hasgill Beck** and onto a grassy track to reach **New House farm**, offering spectacular views back over the reservoir. Turn left in front of the farm and descend a zigzag grassy track to a footbridge over the infant River Hodder, then continue ahead through a kissing gate and right, on past the ruined remains of Collyholme Farm.

Traverse southwest across Copped Hill Clough to the track and turn left, following the flags to a footbridge and onto another track. Head left following the route of the old railway track to the fishing lodge. ▶

Continue along the track all the way to Stocks Reservoir Fly Fishery, where refreshments are available when open. Continue along the track to the Stocks Board House – now housing United Utilities' Bowland Estate Office and straight ahead along a path away from the main track and down to the dam.

This railway was built to carry stone quarried above Cross of Greet Bridge a few kilometres to the north.

49

Looking northwest across the reservoir from the Causeway

Cross the dam and descend the steps, then turn left and left again to join the concessionary path along the eastern shore of the reservoir. Follow the path above the shoreline for almost three kilometres, into scrubby woodland then through a kissing gate on the left towards the end of the field, emerging next to the road.

Continue ahead on the footpath adjacent to the road, emerging onto the road before the **Causeway** at the eastern extremity of the reservoir. Across the causeway, follow the path behind the hedge on your left to your starting point at School Lane car park.

WALK 10

Tarnbrook and the Ward's Stone

Start/finish	Lay-by on Tarnbrook Lane (SD 569 554) or grassy lay-by (SD 580 556)
Distance	12.5km (7¾ miles)
Total ascent	420m
Time	4hr 30min
Map	OS Explorer OL41
Refreshments	The Fleece at Dolphinholme

This epic route explores the remote Upper Wyre Valley, following the Tarnbrook branch of the river up onto the airy 500m plateau forming the roof of the Bowland Fells: the rocky carapace of the Ward's Stone.

Park in the small lay-by on Tarnbrook Lane or the grassy lay-by at SD 580 556 and walk a kilometre and a half or so to the start of the route at the quiet hamlet of Tarnbrook.

Walk east along the lane past Ouzel Bridge for one and a half kilometres.

> **Ouzel Bridge** is named after the rare blackbirds with a distinctive white bib that return to the Bowland Fells each spring. They are easiest to see among the scrub and bushes in the lower-lying valleys in early to mid April, before the leaf cover is fully established.

At the hamlet of **Tarnbrook**, take the permissive footpath on the left over the bridge and into the fields. Follow the track north, climbing steadily up **Tarnsyke Clough** to a gate beside the aqueduct. Through the gate, follow the track left then back right, continuing to climb past the **Luncheon Huts** as the views back west open up over the Fylde plain.

The rocky carapace of the Ward's Stone

After 300 metres, ignore the track off to the right and continue for another 100 metres to take the track off to the left. Contour west across the boulder fields of **Ward's Stone Breast** for 800 metres.

At SD 585 578, the slope to the right broadens into a shallow, wide gulley criss-crossed with faint paths. Aim for the steeper boulder slopes on left-hand side of the gulley, heading just east of north and you will pick up a faint grassy track above the ridge.

Spectacular views open up north to the Three Peaks, the Lakeland fells and out over Morecambe Bay.

It's tough going for a while but the summit weather station comes into view after 500 metres, signposting the way to the summit trig standing amid a carapace of sun-bleached millstone grit. At 560m, **Ward's Stone** summit is the highest point in the Forest of Bowland. ◄

Leave the summit plateau via the eastern edge and past the second, slightly higher, trig point then continue beside a wire fence striking out over the peat hags heading towards the slumbering lioness of Ingleborough. At the junction with a dry stone wall, head half right, keeping the wall on your left.

It's hard going in places, but stick close to the fence and after two and a half kilometres, the fence intersects

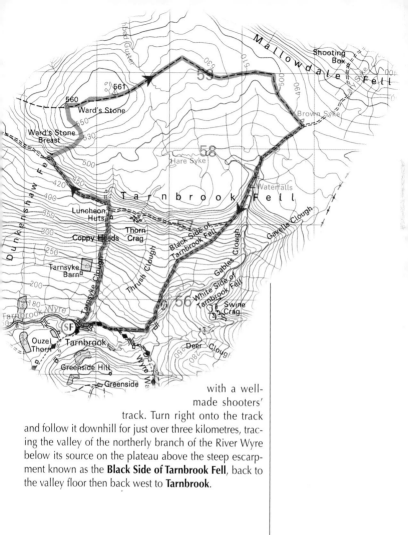

with a well-made shooters' track. Turn right onto the track and follow it downhill for just over three kilometres, tracing the valley of the northerly branch of the River Wyre below its source on the plateau above the steep escarpment known as the **Black Side of Tarnbrook Fell**, back to the valley floor then back west to **Tarnbrook**.

WALK 11

The Upper Wyre Way

Start/finish	Lay-by on Trough of Bowland road (SD 604 538)
Distance	12.5km (7¾ miles)
Total ascent	250m
Time	3hr 30min
Map	OS Explorer OL41
Refreshments	The Fleece at Dolphinholme

This varied route follows the two branches of the Upper River Wyre: the rugged Tarnbrook arm, which rises on the craggy plateaus of the Ward's Stone, and its more sedate southern sibling, the Marshaw Wyre.

The walk begins at **Tower Lodge**. Walk up the track, through woods and take the footpath northwest through a new plantation and up onto the fellside. Continue northwest along the Wyre Way, over a step stile and through a wooden gate. Views open out north up to the Ward's Stone and west over Morecambe Bay.

Descend beside the wall past coppice then between the two outbarns, onto the track and through a gate into a paddock. Head left across the paddock past the farm and across the **footbridge**, then continue over a cattlegrid onto a farm track. Continue along the track and over another cattlegrid then left onto another track.

Continue on the track for 300 metres then through a gate into the hamlet of **Tarnbrook**. After 100 metres, take the footpath left between farm buildings and along a track over a bridge. After the bridge, climb up right above the river, over the next two paddocks and across the farm track via squeeze stiles.

Continue southwest over next three fields, negotiating several rickety stiles and on past a large outbarn. Go over three more stiles and across a footbridge in quick succession and follow the field boundary to the farm. There's one more stile to negotiate – a ladder stile – then go along the track to the road.

Crossing the road, take the footpath opposite and head west across the next three fields to emerge onto the road via the back garden of a cottage. Descend steeply left and over **Tarnbrook Wyre** into the pretty hamlet of **Abbeystead**.

> Nestled in a secluded wooded hollow at the confluence of the two Wyres, **Abbeystead** was briefly the site of a satellite of the Cistercian abbey at Furness in the 12th century. The swampy area downstream of the village was once a reservoir, but fell into disrepair after the mills downstream closed.

Follow the lane through the village and climb for 150 metres to take the footpath on the left past the house and west over the field; go across the beck then left onto a farm track. Follow the track downhill for 200 metres, then round to the right before picking up the foot-path on the

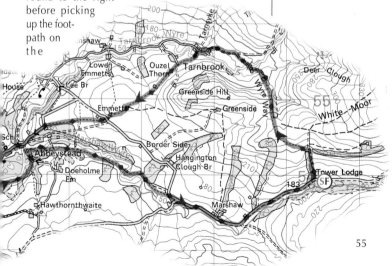

The Trough of Bowland beside the Marshaw Wyre

left alongside the wall above **Abbeystead Reservoir**. Turn left through the gate to cross the river again via a footbridge.

Climb left from the bridge and past the outfall over the distinctive **Weir** then follow the footpath through some woods for 800 metres to emerge onto the road. Caution: the flags and steps here can get very slippery!

Head left over the bridge then right onto the driveway and over a cattlegrid into parkland. Continue east for 200 metres and over a footbridge, continuing east then southeast over the fields skirting Abbeystead House to descend via the steps to reach a footbridge over the **Marshaw Wyre** at the edge of the woods.

With its stands of Scots pine, peaty spate streams and heather-clad moorland, this could be the highlands of Scotland.

Follow the river upstream over the flood meadows for 400 metres then across a field to the road adjacent to Well Brook. Continue east (right) along the road for 150 metres and after the coppice take the concessionary footpath through the gate on the right and follow river upstream through fields for 500 metres to **Marshaw Farm**. ◀ At a cattlegrid, return to the road and follow it upstream for the final kilometre and a half back to the lay-by adjacent to the start of the walk.

WALK 12
Whin Fell and the Brennand Valley

Start/finish	Gravel roadside lay-by on Trough of Bowland Road outside Dunsop Bridge (SD 647 505)
Distance	11.5km (7¼ miles)
Total ascent	360m
Time	4hr
Map	OS Explorer OL41
Refreshments	Puddleducks Café at Dunsop Bridge

Another classic hill walk combining steep climbs, big views and pleasant riverside rambling in the secluded hills and dales at the heart of the Forest of Bowland.

Park on the gravelled area by the roadside about a kilometre and a half along the Trough road from Dunsop Bridge. ▶ Walk northwest up the road until the footpath heads off left across the **Langden Brook**, then take the stile on your right, over the bridge and then over another stile to follow the river upstream on the far bank.

Continue upstream to a paddock and cross the stile keeping the fence on the right. At a little coppice, head left at a fence along the beck then cross the bridge and continue to a kissing gate, turning right down the track to rejoin the road. Head left uphill past farm buildings at **Sykes** and the waterworks to take track off to the right immediately after the barn and climb steadily northeast. Follow the track to a metal gate and, after a stile by a wooden gate and tumbledown mine building, follow the track east through a little coppice. When the wire fence stops, continue straight on with a dry stone wall on your right.

Cross a little beck, then after a dry stone wall heads south, continue east, heading slightly left onto a track,

Alternative parking is available at Sykes, but this means a longer on-road section at the end of your walk.

57

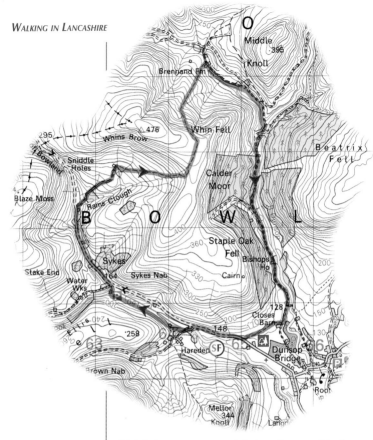

From up on the
plateau, glance over
your shoulder for
a fleeting glimpse
of Morecambe Bay
and south to the
Hodder and Ribble
Valleys, with Pendle
Hill looming large
on the skyline.

which fades to a grassy trod, but continues east to the
edge of the summit plateau. Head for the gap in the wall
where the path takes off up onto the plateau and curves
left. ◀

At the stile, if visibility is good, use the wire fence
as a handrail to reach summit of **Whin Fell** and the trig
point 800 metres to the northwest. It's hard going over the
peat hags, but the views west over the Lune estuary and
Morecambe Bay are epic. The Forest of Bowland extends
all around and to the northeast the Yorkshire Three Peaks
are clearly visible.

Expansive views across Morecambe Bay from the summit of Whin Fell

Retrace your steps to the stile and follow the path as it contours round the edge of summit plateau, curving left to the top of the Ouster Rake – a slightly hair-raising descent across the vertiginous escarpment. ▶

At bottom of the rake, go through the wooden gate and continue northeast towards **Brennand Farm**. The path disappears but stay left and aim for a gate at the top of the field above the farm. Follow the track across fields to reach a ladder stile over a dry stone wall to the left of the farm. Turn right onto the road and continue downhill, along the floor of the beautiful Brennand Valley, keeping right where it forks.

At the confluence of the rivers Brennand and Dunsop, cross to the right-hand bank and follow the river downstream for the next two and a half kilometres. At a footbridge, stay right on the metalled road and, just before the cattle grid at **Closes Barn**, bear right into the field and follow the path round the back of the barn and over a stone stile next to an iron gate. Continue across the field, parallel to the dry stone wall, passing farm buildings on your left, to a gate next to a fingerpost. Turn right onto the road and walk the final 200 metres back to your car.

In winter, this north-facing slope never sees the sun, so beware of ice and tread carefully.

WALK 13

Whitendale Hanging Stones

Start/finish	Single parking space next to gate (SD 692 547), 100m southeast of gate onto access land
Distance	15.5km (9½ miles)
Total ascent	550m
Time	5hr
Map	OS Explorer OL41
Refreshments	Riverbank Tearooms, Slaidburn
Parking	If the single space is taken, park further down the lane

Starting just outside the picturesque stone village of Slaidburn, this walk climbs up onto the central plateau of Bowland via a Roman Road, through the pretty valley of Croasdale and returns via the geographical centre of the United Kingdom and the beautiful Whitendale Valley.

Walk uphill and through a gate onto a track and straight on past the RAF memorial, following the signpost to Hornby Road. Follow the track round to the left, climbing steadily, then more steeply along the lip of the valley to reach the white Tercet Stone to the right of the track.

Tercet Stones are the distinctive waymarkers that denote The Lancashire Witches' Way. They were installed along the long-distance footpath between Lancaster and Clitheroe to mark the 400th anniversary of the Lancashire Witch Trials. Each is inscribed with a poem by the then Poet Laureate Carol Ann Duffy, telling the story of the witches along the route of their final journey across the moors to meet their fate at the Lancaster Assizes.

If you're lucky, you might spot hen harriers, merlin or ring ouzel near the Rowan trees further up the track.

◄ Continue past the tercet post, climbing steadily to the skyline. As the track levels out, go through the gate

One of the tercet posts marking the Lancashire Witches Way

and continue northwest along the route of the Roman Road, beneath the rocky knoll of Wolfhole Crag away to the west.

Continue along the track for 800 metres, past the faint path on left into Whitendale and through another gate. At the next gate (SD 652 587), follow the fence left to cross the head of the valley.

The next stretch is very boggy after heavy rain and requires careful negotiation. At Greenhole Spring, the Lakeland fells appear to the north. ▶

Continue beside the fence to the kissing gate at the junction of the fences at SD 641 576. At 480m, the views open up massively to the north and east, taking in the Lakeland fells, the Howgills and the Yorkshire Three Peaks. It's a climb of around 800 metres over moorland to reach the summit of Wolfhole Crag, but worth the detour on a clear day.

The route descends left along the fence line. Follow the fence line southeast, descending along the broad ridge of **Brown Syke Hill** to the stones at White Crag then south for 800 metres to **Whitendale Hanging Stones**.

Across the fence, the seaside soundtrack comes courtesy of several thousand Herring gulls forming the largest inland gull colony in Britain.

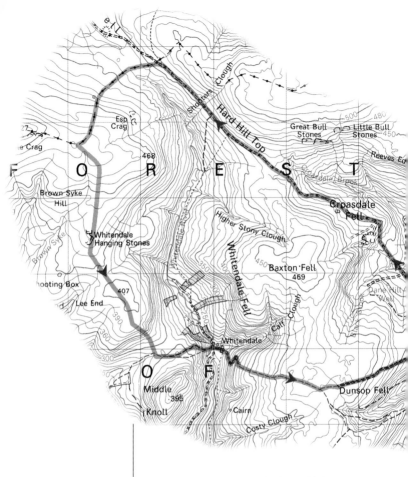

Using the gravitational method to establish Britain's centre of gravity, Ordnance Survey calculated that the **geographical centre of Great Britain** (including 401 associated islands) lies at SD 6419 5654, in the field northwest of Whitendale Hanging Stones.

Beyond the stones, follow the fence southeast over Far Pasture Brow and descend into Whitendale. It's an initially steep descent, so it pays to zigzag down to the dry stone wall at foot of the scarp.

Head for the 'gate' at the intersection of two dry stone walls and follow a faint path through some rushes to the far side of the pond. Then follow the bridleway left to a gate and descend to join the track into **Whitendale**. Cross the footbridge and continue between the farm buildings on a track heading east. Fork right up a grassy trod before a concrete bridge and zigzag steeply up onto open moorland.

At the top of the zigzag, fork right again and climb steadily up to the plateau. From the cairn, follow the yellow marker posts southeast to a gate. Go through the gate and east along a faint path to the left, on the side of **Dunsop Fell**. After 400 metres, look for a grassy trod running east 100 metres south of the dry stone wall. Follow this track for just over one and a half kilometres back to the starting point at the edge of access land.

Inscription on a Tercet Stone

63

WALK 14
Whitewell and the Upper Hodder Valley

Start/finish	Car park outside the Inn at Whitewell (SD 659 468)
Distance	13km (8 miles)
Total ascent	335m
Time	4hr
Map	OS Explorer OL41
Refreshments	The Inn at Whitewell

The perfect precursor to a hearty lunch at one of Lancashire's most iconic country inns – the Inn at Whitewell. This walk climbs high above the Hodder for superb views up the valley before returning along the river.

The view north from Burholme Bridge

Park at the Inn at **Whitewell** and walk down past the **chapel** to the **River Hodder**, following it downstream to cross at the stepping stones. On the far bank, follow the path uphill to **New Laund farm** through the farmyard then half left at a fingerpost by the cheese press, signposted Tunstall Ings.

Follow the grassy track, contouring anti-clockwise around the base of **New Laund Hill**. At the northern side of the hill, join the road going left then turn right over a stile onto the footpath, heading west to the farmhouse.

Multiple archaeological digs have uncovered evidence of two distinct phases of **Neolithic occupation** at New Laund Hill. Nomadic herders may have used the lower plateau as a temporary camp, while early pastoralists established a more permanent settlement on the upper plateau offering commanding views of the valley.

Just before the farmhouse, turn right following the track as it climbs and twists and turns up on to the fells. After 500 metres, take the

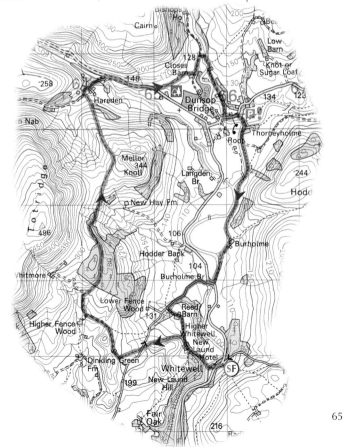

The Inn at Whitewell

Much of the pine plantation has been recently felled, revealing superb views up the Hodder Valley from the summit.

bridleway off to the right through a gate into **Lower Fence Wood**.

◀ Continue north on the path running left of **Mellor Knoll** then descend through Riggs Plantation to the farm at **Hareden** to join the Trough of Bowland road and head right towards **Dunsop Bridge**.

Continue along the road for 400 metres then, after a cattle grid, take the footpath on the left and head across fields to **Closes Barn**. Turn left onto a track to cross a footbridge, then head right along a track into Dunsop Bridge.

Head left on the road through the village, then right into the driveway of **Thorneyholme Hall**. Cross the river again on the footbridge and then turn immediately right to continue along the riverbank.

Follow the path through fields downstream to **Burholme** and take a right turn through the farmyard onto a footpath (not track). This takes you through the fields to rejoin the road and cross the bridge. Follow the road uphill and, after 500 metres, take the footpath along the track on the left back to New Laund Farm. Then it's a case of retracing your route across the stepping stones back to the Inn at **Whitewell**.

WALK 15

Glasson, Cockersand Abbey and Conder Green

Start/finish	Car park outside the Stork Inn, Conder Green (SD 459 559)
Distance	13.5km (8¼ miles)
Total ascent	80m
Time	3hr 30min
Map	OS Explorer 296
Refreshments	Glasson Dock, The Mill at Conder Green
Public transport	Bus 89 from Lancaster

This circular coastal route starts in the quirky little port of Glasson Dock and follows the southern bank of the Lune estuary past the remains of Cockersand Abbey before returning via the Lancaster Canal.

From the car park, turn left into the lane heading west then left again onto the coast path and over the footbridge. Continue along the coast path beside the road (B5290) for 800 metres into Glasson Dock, then turn left over the

The main basin at Glasson Dock

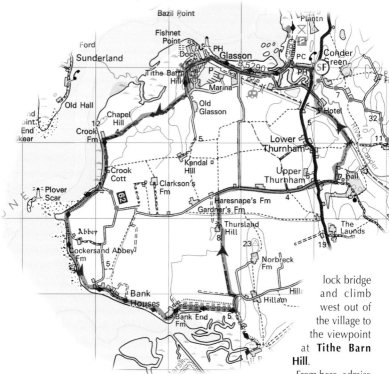

lock bridge and climb west out of the village to the viewpoint at **Tithe Barn Hill**.

From here, admire the views out over the mouth of the Lune to Morecambe Bay. Behind, to the east, are the hills of the Forest of Bowland, while the Lakeland fells brood on the northern horizon.

Follow the road south for 200 metres then cross the road and take the bridleway on your right for just over a kilometre, across farmland to the coast. At the coast, head left along the lane and continue south then south-west for 800 metres past the Victorian Abbey Lighthouse at **Plover Scar**.

The **Abbey Lighthouse** is an elegant, octagonal stone structure and originally formed the lower light of a pair of navigational lights indicating the entry to the main shipping channel up the Lune.

The taller light was decommissioned in the 80s, but the light on Plover Scar remains active – despite sustaining extensive damage after being hit by a freighter in 2016.

Navigation buoy on the coast path with the Abbey Lighthouse in the distance

After the coastline swings back to the south, a short detour inland leads to the remains of 12th century **Cockersand Abbey**, though all that remains of this Premonstratensian abbey and hospital is the Grade 1 listed vaulted chapter house. Continue south along the coast and beside the lookout tower, follow the coast path back east along the beach.

At the road junction, follow the road round to the left through **Bank Houses** and then take the bridleway off to the left at **Bank End Farm**. Follow the track round to the right and continue along the coast path, past the caravan parks then along the farm lane for just under a kilometre. ▸

This salt marsh is grazed by sheep, producing lean and delicately flavoured salt-marsh lamb.

At the junction, follow the road round to the left then, after 150 metres, take the bridleway on the left.

Plover Scar light from Cockersand Abbey

Follow the bridleway round to right and continue north to **Thursland Hill farm**. Go left through the gate and straight on past the pond, over the footbridge and into Moss Lane.

Head right along the lane for just over a kilometre, then cross the main road and go right for 20 metres before taking the footpath left along the driveway of Thurnham **Hall**. At the car park, head left across in front of the hall, through the grounds to a green lane and over a stile.

Cross the field and head over the bridge to the towpath on the far side of the canal. Continue left (north) along the canal. At the **Hotel** by the locks, walk through the car park and along the drive back to the road. Head left then right over the bridge (caution: traffic!) to return to the car park.

WALK 16

Gragareth – Lancashire's county top

Start/finish	Ireby (SD 654 756)
Distance	13.5km (8¼ miles)
Total ascent	520m
Time	5hr
Map	OS Explorer OL2
Refreshments	Ingleton or Kirkby Lonsdale
Parking	Limited, but there is room for one car on grass opposite footpath sign at top of Ireby (SD 654 756)

A demanding hike to the county highpoint – a lofty Lancastrian outpost in the border country between the Howgill fells and the rugged limestone uplands of the Yorkshire Dales.

Cross the stile and head northwest on the footpath uphill, going left through a gate before continuing to the farm alongside the wall. Cross the ladder stile then go through the gate and right onto the track. Continue north, climbing gently past the rhododendrons of the Leck Hall Estate. At the junction with the road (east of **Fellside Barn**), turn right, heading uphill for 800 metres onto the side of **Leck Fell**.

At SD 670 786 it's worth going through the gate on the right to wander 50 metres to **Lost John's Cave**, where a stream disappears into the subterranean labyrinth of cave systems in the permeable limestone.

There are several **Caves of Gragareth**. This route passes noted limestone potholes like Lost John's Cave and Ireby Fell Caverns, but the most accessible is Yordas Cave, below the north-eastern flank.

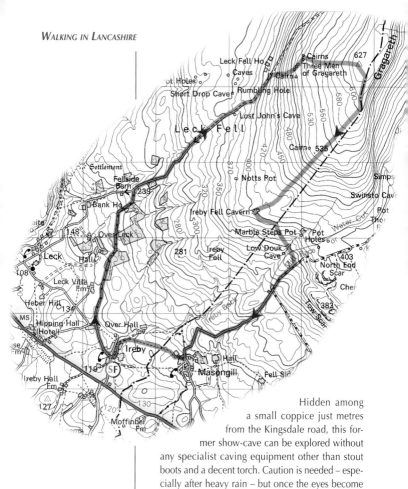

Hidden among a small coppice just metres from the Kingsdale road, this former show-cave can be explored without any specialist caving equipment other than stout boots and a decent torch. Caution is needed – especially after heavy rain – but once the eyes become accustomed to the gloom, a cathedral-like chamber, complete with some bizarre rock formations and a subterranean stream, are revealed.

After another 500 metres, take the gate on the right at SD 675 791 on to access land and follow the faint grassy path through the boulder field and directly up the steep escarpment to the ridge. It's not as bad as it looks and

after five minutes' determined ascent, a cairn and shelter appear on the skyline. A line of prominent cairns known as the **Three Men of Gragareth** come into view shortly after. Head directly for them.

In poor visibility, simply continue just north of east to the edge of the plateau, then contour round to meet the men at SD 671 793. ▸

No one seems to know how old **The Three Men of Gragareth** are, but they are definitely suffering from a bit of middle-aged spread! Further uphill lie the Three Men's female companions: the Three Women of Gragareth. These slender and elegantly sculpted structures are more impressive than their male counterparts.

From the Three Men, a path now runs almost due east, climbing steadily to the summit trig of **Gragareth**.

At 627m, **Gragareth** is the highest point in Lancashire and the views from the top stretch over to Great Coum, Ingleborough, Whernside and

*The Three Men
of Gragareth*

There is a line of smaller cairns on the edge of the plateau, but the Three Men rise out of a rather ramshackle scree pile a little further along.

across Morecambe Bay to the Furness peninsulas. On a clear day, Lancashire's former highpoint of Coniston Old Man is just visible on the horizon to the north-west.

Head southeast to the wall and follow it south. Go over the ladder stile and follow the right side of the wall south along the ridge. On the left lies the delightfully remote valley of Kingsdale and, across the valley, Yorkshire's highest point – the 736m summit of Whernside.

At the next wall junction, climb over the low section of dry stone wall in the corner of the field and continue south along the wall. At the next junction of walls, go through the gap and pick up a faint track heading downhill between the two walls.

Where the gradient levels off, follow the deepening gulley downhill to **Ireby Fell Cavern**. Stay on the right of the gulley, following the faint path around the lip. From the cavern entrance at SD 674 773, contour southeast to pick up the path to the stile over the wall at SD 677 772.

Cross the wall and descend on the faint path to the Turbary Road. Turn right and head downhill onto Masongill Fell Lane and onwards into **Masongill** then take footpath on the right opposite the telephone box. Cross three fields then over the stile to join track back into **Ireby**.

Looking up Kingsdale to Whernside

WALK 17
Kirkby Lonsdale and Whittington

Start/finish	Market Place, Kirkby Lonsdale (SD 611 786)
Distance	10km (6¼ miles)
Total ascent	170m
Time	3hr
Map	OS Explorer OL2
Refreshments	Kirkby Lonsdale
Public transport	8, 9 from Lancaster; 580 from Settle; 567 from Kendal.
Parking	Limited in the Market Place, but there are a number of pay and display car parks in the town

Most of this delightful route along the Lune Valley lies in Lancashire, but we make no apologies for the fact that the walk starts and finishes in the picture postcard market town of Kirkby Lonsdale, which – strictly speaking – is in Cumbria.

From the market square, head north along Main Street, then left along Market Street and right at The Sun, through pretty St Mary's churchyard, following signs for Ruskin's View.

At the riverside path, head left to admire the view, then track back and descend the steep steps to follow the riverside path to Devil's Bridge. ▶

> If the footpath is closed due to high water levels, leave the churchyard into Swinemarket and descend to the river via Mill Brow.

Ruskin's View, offering vistas up the Lune Valley towards the Howgill fells, is just a five-minute walk from the market square in the town centre. John Ruskin himself described the view as one of the most naturally divine places in the whole of Europe.

At Devil's Bridge, stay on the town side of the river, taking the footpath that heads downstream along the

riverbank. Cross the busy A65 with care and continue downstream along the side of the River Lune.

At the pipeline bridge, climb to the right of the parapet to avoid an eroded bank and go over a stile beside a metal gate. Continue downstream over two more stiles to rejoin the riverbank, then – at the stile where the path is badly eroded – climb away from bank and continue along the field boundary.

At the shed, just after the fishing pier that protrudes into the river, go half right over a cattle grid and along a track for 100 metres, then turn right and follow the track northwest into **Whittington**.

On reaching the road in the village, turn left and follow with care for 75 metres before crossing the road and taking the footpath just before the gatehouse. Follow this path over parkland then across a paddock and through the churchyard into the village.

Cross the road and take the lane heading steeply uphill after the post box. ◄

As the gradient eases, look right for dramatic views of Ingleborough.

Just after the long, low house at the brow of the hill, take the footpath on the right and continue past the plantation next to **Sellet Hall** to a stile in the hedge. Cross the stile and continue east along a field boundary to a green gate in the hedge. Skirt the edge of the farm at **Sellet Mill** via another two green gates to join a bridleway heading north beside the beck.

The bridleway actually merges with the riverbed and the rocks are potentially wet and slippery after very heavy rain, but with appropriate footwear, tread carefully and it is no more difficult than a rocky mountain path.

After 150 metres, the bridleway leaves the streambed and follows a holloway to join a lane on the outskirts of **Kirkby Lonsdale**. Go through the kissing gate and take the footpath signposted Devil's Bridge across a paddock and through an iron gate.

Continue north across some fields and then a rugby pitch, then cross the A65 and head past the tennis courts. Turn right along Biggins Road and into town via Mitchelgate and left into Main Street to return to the market square.

WALK 18
Sunderland Point

Start/finish	Overton at Ship Hotel car park (SD 433 580)
Distance	11km (7 miles)
Total ascent	70m
Time	3hr
Map	OS Explorer 296
Refreshments	Overton
Public transport	1 or 1A from Lancaster to Overton
Parking	Also available at the Globe Hotel (SD 433 579)
Warning	Be aware of the tides. Don't attempt to cross the causeway within two hours of high spring tides.

This wonderfully wild walk explores the windswept expanses of the salt marshes and the lonely Sunderland Peninsula, guarding the northern approaches to the Lune estuary.

Sunderland Point from Bazil Point

From the crossroads in the centre of the village, follow Chapel Lane round left and then right and continue south along the lane out of the village for 400 metres. Continue straight on down the track then the footpath to the coast at Fiskes Point.

Turn right and follow the coastal path around **Bazil Point**. Continue north on the beach then up onto a footpath along the inlet to meet the causeway road.

Turn left along the causeway, heading towards Sunderland.

Sunderland is regularly cut off by high tides and care is needed to cross the **Causeway** safely. Use the sea wall road 200 metres to the north if the Causeway is cut off. The causeway floods at both ends, so don't be tempted to hang around in the middle admiring the expansive coastal views, delightful though they are.

Continue south along road over Lades Marsh to **Sunderland** and onwards through the pretty village towards the tip of the peninsula.

*The plaque and poem
on Sambo's Grave*

The footpath peters out after the village, but as long as the tides permit, it is possible to walk all the way round **Sunderland Point** along the beach. If in doubt, take the shortcut along the bridleway that leads out of the village to the western shore.

The coastal route fetches up at the pretty new memorial at Sambo's Grave – complete with wildlife hide and rather amazing horizon observation chamber, that projects an image of the coast onto a screen inside. It's great for uniquely Instagrammable selfies.

Sambo's Grave is the burial site of to a young African servant, who died shortly after arriving from the West Indies with his master in 1736. He was buried in an unmarked grave, largely forgotten until 1796, when a poem was written about him. Today, Sambo's Grave is a poignant reminder of the Port of Lancaster's role in the slave trade.

Continue north along the high water mark then along the track to the car park at **Potts' Corner** and follow the road inland (right) as it zigzags across farmland. After 500 metres, take the footpath on the right and continue past a workshop, heading east to Trailhome Road. In the next field, head straight across to join a track skirting left of **Trumley Farm**.

Continue east along the path for 250 metres, then turn left into a lane beside the sea wall. Go through a gate up onto the sea wall around top of inlet to return to **Overton**.

WALK 19

Silverdale and Warton Crag

Start/finish	Silverdale station (SD 476 751)
Distance	12.5km (7¾ miles)
Total ascent	280m
Time	4hr
Map	OS Explorer OL7
Refreshments	Leighton Moss Visitor Centre or Wolf House Gallery, Silverdale
Public transport	Northern Rail Cumbria Coast Line; Trains from Lancaster

This splendid walk starts in a nature reserve and climbs the coastal limestone knoll of Warton Crag before returning via salt marshes on the edge of Morecambe Bay.

From the railway station, head left (south) and take first the lane on the left past RSPB Leighton Moss **Visitor Centre**. Walk along the road for 400 metres before taking the bridleway to Home Farm on the right. Follow the gravelled path between the reeds at **Leighton Moss** and maybe pop into the hide for a peek at the birdlife. ▶

In spring listen out for the booming call of the bittern, which carries for miles across the reserve.

Leaving the marshes, follow the farm track towards the buildings, through two gates and past a farmhouse B&B, contouring round the base of the wooded crag. Continue along a metalled road past **Leighton Hall** and then peel off left up the hill to the skyline.

The elegant edifice of **Leighton Hall** was the work of local furniture magnate Richard Gillow, who reshaped it in the Gothic style in the early 19th century. It is furnished with some exquisite pieces acquired by the Gillow clan and has remained in the family ever since.

Leighton Hall

It's an Arthurian kind of place with dappled light playing on the moss-cloaked drystone walls.

It's a short steep haul but there are benches at the top offering great views over the parkland and across the estuary to Grange. Turn right and follow the top of the ridge south following the line of an ancient wall punctuated by a large erratic boulder.

Go through the gate and along the well-made forest track descending slightly to the road and turn right down the hill. Follow the road round to the left, ignoring footpaths either side, and continue downhill.

After a shallow bend, just after 30mph signs, take a footpath on the right climbing very steeply up into woods. ◄ Continue climbing for 400 metres until the track levels out.

After 500 metres, follow the footpath to the summit off to the left, clearly marked with a sign for the nature reserve through the gate. Continue climbing towards the summit trig as the path narrows and gets quite overgrown near the top. Emerge from the trees into a glade on the summit of **Warton Crag**, with a beacon and superb views out over the bay.

Leave the summit by the path heading northwest to regain the bridleway. Go through a wooden gate and continue straight on. At the second wooden gate, go left along the bridleway and, after a gentle

descent of about 800 metres, turn right onto a lane. After 500 metres on the lane, follow the main road round to the left and join the **Lancashire Coastal Way** where it heads left under the railway.

The smelting kiln chimney at Jenny Brown's Point

Cross the little bridge and continue over salt marsh, then along the foot of a wooded crag towards the smelting kiln chimney.

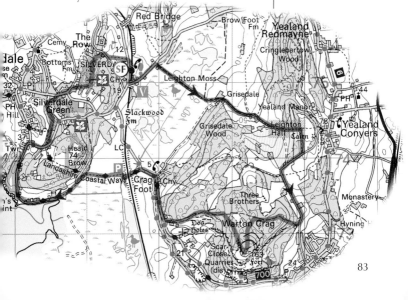

Wander across the limestone slabs to join the met-alled coast road beyond the cottages and stay on the road past Jenny Brown's point towards Silverdale.

The preponderance of limestone hereabouts leads most visitors to conclude that that the chimney near **Jenny Brown's point** is part of a limekiln; but actually, this listed structure is believed to belong to a short-lived copper smelting plant on the site.

Beyond **Lindeth Tower**, head right along Hollins Lane then take footpath left into the National Trust woodland. Follow the path to the right into a clearing, then follow the sign for **Silverdale Green** via the Chase.

When the footpath joins the lane, turn right and continue for 200 metres before taking the road left sign-posted for Burton Well.

Continue past the well into Lambert's meadow, heading right over a footbridge and into woodland again. Climb steeply up the steps before the path levels out just before meeting the road. Turn right for 100 metres along the road, then take the footpath left across a golf course and back to **Silverdale station** via a stile next to a gate to the greenkeeper's shed.

Sheep grazing on the saltmarsh near Jenny Brown's Point

WALK 20

*Easington Fell and Beacon Hill
from Grindleton*

Start/finish	The Duke of York Inn, Grindleton (SD 759 455)
Distance	12.5km (7¾ miles)
Total ascent	400m
Time	4hr
Map	OS Explorer OL41
Refreshments	The Spread Eagle, Sawley
Public transport	Clitheroe station, then number 3 Clitheroe Sawley Circular bus (every two hours) from Interchange

Starting out as a pleasant valley stroll, this route climbs steadily up onto the open fells and the views that unfold over the Hodder Valley and into the Yorkshire Dales are outstanding.

From the Duke of York Inn, which stands on the cross roads at centre of Grindleton village, walk west to Weaver's Cottages then hop right, over a stile into Greendale Wood. Follow the footpath over a footbridge then turn left at the perimeter of the wood. At the edge of the wood, continue southwest along the field boundary to the farm then over a stile and right onto Green Lane. Follow this track for almost three kilometres as it climbs steadily up onto the fellside. ▶ Beyond the farmhouse, ignore the first farm track off to the left, but take the second left instead, climbing again towards Simpshey Hill. Beyond Cob Manor, Simpshey appears ahead. Through the gate at the top of the track, take a stile left and follow the path downhill, across a footbridge, before climbing half left past a ruined barn.

Join a grassy track following the bridleway as it the skirts the base of hill and continues climbing north to turn left onto gravel logging track. The track climbs past

In May, the beech woods to the left are a glorious riot of spring colour – shot through with bluebells and ramsons (wild garlic), and echoing to a rousing chorus of birdsong.

Simpshey Hill seen from the coppice above Cob Manor

a conifer plantation up onto the open fellside to a cairn on the skyline.

From the cairn, head half left to the corner of the plantation, following a faint path northeast along the perimeter. Climb over a rusty gate with care and head over the tumbledown wall then follow it northeast for 400 metres to the summit of **Easington Fell**. ◄

To the north, the Bowland Fells dominate the north-western skyline and, once over the brow, the Yorkshire Three Peaks suddenly appear.

Follow the wall around the plantation as it winds back southeast. Where the gradient eases, head half left to a gate then left on a permissive path alongside a wall, heading southeast. After the wall ends, continue to the corner of the field and turn right over the stile to continue east on a permissive path, then half right following a fire-break into the plantation.

This ancient track is so named owing to its alignment, which exposed shepherds and other travellers to cold, north-easterly winds which would scour the ridgeline in winter.

At the far edge of the plantation, join the wonderfully named Shivering Ginnel, heading northeast. ◄ Continue straight over the stile, heading for the trig point on the summit of **Beacon Hill**. The footpath passes to the left of the trig and continues to a lane. Turn right and continue along the lane for 300 metres before taking a stile on the left. Continue across the field to another stile then onto the track for a brief stretch, before taking the footpath

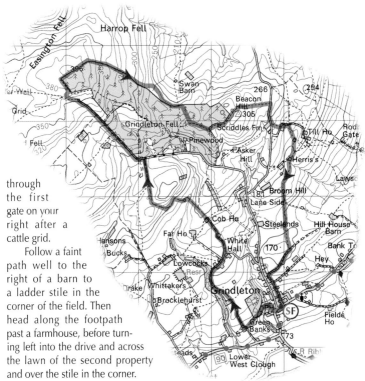

through the first gate on your right after a cattle grid.

Follow a faint path well to the right of a barn to a ladder stile in the corner of the field. Then head along the footpath past a farmhouse, before turning left into the drive and across the lawn of the second property and over the stile in the corner.

Continue over a stile downhill into the corner of the field, then over a succession of stiles and a footbridge, continuing south over the fields to a grassy track heading right above Far Lathe. Follow this southwest to the edge of the village then, when you reach the back yard of the first house, turn left and follow the footpath downhill. Continue down through the back streets before heading right into the centre of **Grindleton**.

WALK 21
The Bowland Traverse

Start	Wennington (SD 617 699)
Finish	Giggleswick (SD 803 629)
Distance	45.5km (28½ miles) (Day 1: 26.5km, Day 2: 19km)
Total ascent	1175m (Day 1: 750m, Day 2: 425m)
Time	2 days (Day 1: 8hr, Day 2: 6hr)

Alfred Wainwright described the Hornby Road between Slaidburn and Wray as 'the best moorland walk in England'. I've included this stunning route within a longer two-day hike across the Bowland Fells, as it showcases some of the area's scenic highlights.

Crossing the lonely uplands at the heart of the Forest of Bowland, over 45 kilometres, this exhilarating trek takes in some of the most spectacular views in this Area of Outstanding Natural Beauty. The daily distances are manageable year-round and navigation is fairly straightforward; with stations at either end of the route, the logistics of getting back to the start point are simple. Overnight accommodation is available at the Hark to Bounty (www.harktobounty.co.uk) or the YHA in Slaidburn, or by taking a short detour, the bunkhouse or luxury B&B at Dalehouse Barn above Stocks Reservoir (www.dalehouse.co.uk).

Day 1: Wennington to Slaidburn (26.5km, 8hr)

From the station car park, turn left then left again over the railway bridge and up Old Moor Road, taking the footpath on the right after 200 metres. Head half left across the field to a gate beneath some trees, then join the drive that runs past the farm and turn right through two gates and into a meadow.

Cross the meadow to a gate, then head across the next meadow to a stile which is to the left of a barn at **Wennington Old Farm**. Go into the woods, through a

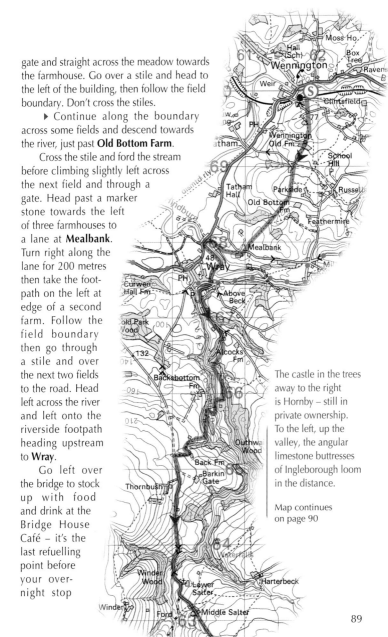

gate and straight across the meadow towards the farmhouse. Go over a stile and head to the left of the building, then follow the field boundary. Don't cross the stiles.

▶ Continue along the boundary across some fields and descend towards the river, just past **Old Bottom Farm**.

Cross the stile and ford the stream before climbing slightly left across the next field and through a gate. Head past a marker stone towards the left of three farmhouses to a lane at **Mealbank**. Turn right along the lane for 200 metres then take the footpath on the left at edge of a second farm. Follow the field boundary then go through a stile and over the next two fields to the road. Head left across the river and left onto the riverside footpath heading upstream to **Wray**.

Go left over the bridge to stock up with food and drink at the Bridge House Café – it's the last refuelling point before your overnight stop

The castle in the trees away to the right is Hornby – still in private ownership. To the left, up the valley, the angular limestone buttresses of Ingleborough loom in the distance.

Map continues on page 90

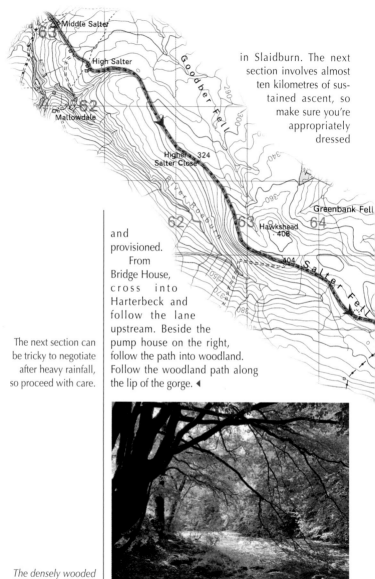

in Slaidburn. The next section involves almost ten kilometres of sustained ascent, so make sure you're appropriately dressed and provisioned.

From Bridge House, cross into Harterbeck and follow the lane upstream. Beside the pump house on the right, follow the path into woodland. Follow the woodland path along the lip of the gorge. ◀

The next section can be tricky to negotiate after heavy rainfall, so proceed with care.

The densely wooded valley of Roeburndale

The densely wooded gorge of Roeburndale is one of the few remnants of Littoral Atlantic Rainforest in Lancashire. It's the closest thing we have to jungle in Western Europe and a precious ecosystem with a rare microclimate.

In 1967, the farming communities eking out an existence in this secluded valley were devastated as a raging torrent of floodwater destroyed everything in its path following a torrential summer downpour as a storm broke over the fells. Cattle, barns and bridges were all swept away in **The Great Flood**: a precursor to the extreme flooding that is now a regular occurrence in the Lune catchment. Preserving these woodlands, and the peat on the fells above, is likely to be critical in preventing similar devastation in the future.

Descend with care on the steep section to the riverside then continue upstream to a clearing and on to the bridge. Cross to the right-hand bank, climbing steeply through the wood-

Map continues on page 93

land and passing tumbledown sheds to join a rough track zigzagging up past the outdoors study centre, then right over a stile, climbing steeply

The Hornby Road climbs towards Salter Fell

through woodland and over the fields to the farms and on to the lane.

At the lane, head left for one and a half kilometres to Barkin Bridge. ◄ Continue along the road for another kilometre and a half to **High Salter Farm**, then onto the gravel track beyond the farm and through a gate onto the Hornby Road.

Stay with this track for the next 11 kilometres as it traverses the gritstone heart of Bowland. After the initial climb, the gradient eases. To the right, the gnarly tor of Wolfhole Crag and then the lonely valley of Whitendale meanders deeper into the heart of Bowland. Above this remote valley lies the geographical centre of Great Britain, at Whitendale Hanging stones.

Continue through the occasional gate to the high point of the trail, where views open out into the Hodder and Ribble Valleys. Descend above the pretty valley of Croasdale, passing one of the Tercet Stones marking the Lancashire Witches' Way as the 'Big End' of Pendle comes into view.

At a marker post (SD 688 557), above an out-barn with enclosures, take the footpath left signposted Croasdale. ◄

Now the views open out north to the Three Peaks and south over the Bowland Fells.

This section can get boggy after heavy rain, but don't be deterred, the path is there!

Descend via a grassy path through a gate following yellow marker posts and wooden walkways left down to the river. Follow the river downstream via the markers and through a gate to cross further downstream via a footbridge. Climb the far bank and go through a gate to cross the field half right towards woods.

Join the track downhill then right along a track past **Croasdale House** for 400 metres then, after some large barns depart half right over the field and through a kissing gate. Continue to left of **Shay House**, across a succession of fields and over a hill heading southeast via the coppice to descend to a lane. Follow the lane downhill into **Slaidburn**.

Day 2: Slaidburn to Giggleswick (19km, 6hr)

From **Slaidburn**, head left past the war memorial and continue over the bridge, taking the footpath on the right alongside the river to the ford, before heading left across the field via a grassy track and through some gates. Continue alongside the wall to join the farm track and continue across the river at **Holmehead Bridge**.

Follow the path upstream then pick up a track for 400 metres to **Hammerton Hall**. Continue half right on the track, then take the left-hand fork through a gate, climbing up with a wall on your right. Go through another gate and across a field to a coppice and follow

a concessionary path left to cross a stile and descend to the track heading right along the bank of **Stocks Reservoir**.

Continue along the bank for just under two and a half kilometres to reach the causeway at the eastern edge of the reservoir. Turn left into road and cross the **Causeway**, then follow the footpath on the left of the road for 250 metres before turning right and across the road onto a footpath into the forest.

Gisburn Forest is criss-crossed with paths and cycle tracks. Our route follows Bottoms Beck for almost two and a half kilometres then continues to Whelp Stone Crag. Stick to the signed footpaths and logging tracks and you shouldn't get lost.

Follow the yellow marker posts and keep heading roughly northeast for almost two and a half kilometres and you will reach a bridge where several trails converge. Cross the bridge and follow the track round to the right for 400 metres, then follow the path on the left for another 400 metres before heading right on a faint path along the edge of a clear-felled area.

After 800 metres of climbing, join a track heading left and continue heading north past a barn. Follow this track north for 800 metres then northeast for another 800 metres to emerge below the craggy outcrop of the Whelpstones.

Follow the well-worn path to the right of the Whelpstones and through the gate, then climb left to reach the trig point at the summit of **Whelp Stone Crag**. ▶

From the trig point, follow a faint path northeast along the edge of an outcrop then follow the edge of the forest northwest to a collapsed wall line at SD 759 603. This is access land and the route is very faint and boggy in places, but use the wall as a hand rail and you will be fine. Head right along the grassed-over wall line towards trees on the skyline and through squeeze the stile.

Admire the views over the limestone landscapes of the Lancashire-Yorkshire borderlands.

Map continues on page 96

Continue across the next field and stay on the edge of the rougher, unimproved access land across a sequence

Looking across the Ribble Valley to the Limestone Country of the Dales

of stone stiles for another 800 metres to reach the beck. The path is faint and boggy in places, but keep heading towards the limestone outcrops above Settle in the distance and you will reach a grassy track that descends into a shallow ghyll.

Continue along a track, taking the middle of the three

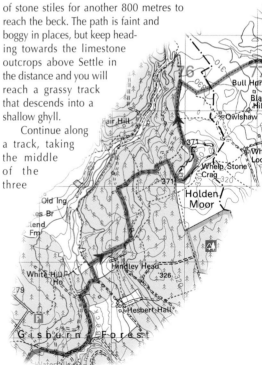

gates beyond the ghyll and continue straight ahead. At the crossroads beside a corrugated chicken hut, head slightly left, through the first farm, and across a stream to a lane. Continue right along the lane past the farm at **Sheep Wash** for 500 metres and take the second footpath on the left.

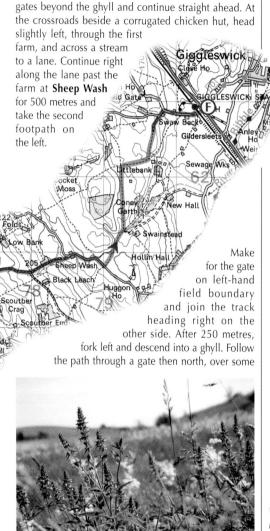

Make for the gate on left-hand field boundary and join the track heading right on the other side. After 250 metres, fork left and descend into a ghyll. Follow the path through a gate then north, over some

Wildflower meadows beside Stocks Reservoir

The verdant pastureland of the Hodder Valley

craggy pasture, and through a gap in the wall then left of barn to join the green lane. Head right down this rather overgrown holloway, taking a footpath on the left after 400 metres.

Go through three rather awkward gates and follow the boundary wall then the telegraph poles to another green lane. Continue right down the lane then left on the footpath beside the main road to the station at **Giggleswick**.

The Bowland Fells seen from Longridge Fell (Walk 23)

WALK 22

Hurst Green and Ribchester

Start/finish	The Shireburn Arms, Hurst Green (SD 685 379)
Distance	8.5km (5¼ miles)
Total ascent	170m
Time	3hr
Map	OS Explorer OL41
Refreshments	The Shireburn Arms
Public transport	5, 5A Chipping to Clitheroe

This three-hour riverside ramble starts from The Shireburn Arms and descends through farmland to the River Ribble, crossing the beautifully restored footbridge at Dinckley, then following the river downstream to re-cross at the Roman settlement of Ribchester and return through the woods.

From the front door of the pub at **Hurst Green**, turn left and after 25 metres take the farm track on the left along Lambing Clough Lane. Descend past the houses and over the cattle grids for 800 metres and follow the track between the farm buildings. Cross the stile on the left to follow the footpath along the edge of the woods to the newly restored footbridge over the **River Ribble**.

Storm Desmond wrecked the original suspension bridge here back in 2015 and its replacement took four years to complete. The original bridge support pillars were retained, but the actual footway has been raised by two metres to protect it from damage in future floods.

Cross the river then turn right and follow the far bank for 800 metres to **Marles Wood**. After another 400 metres through the woods, where the river widens into a lagoon,

ignore the concessionary path to left and
continue straight on through the woods
to the lane.

Turn right along the lane and
continue past **Salesbury Hall**, following the lane for just
over one kilometre
to the stone

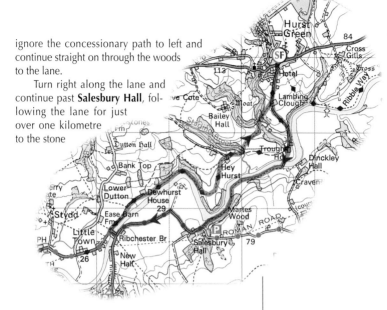

bridge at Ribchester. Cross the bridge and turn right
along the track following the Ribble Way footpath.

> As its name suggests, **Ribchester** has Roman origins.
> The Romans established a cavalry fort at Ribchester
> almost 2000 years ago – part of a network of
> defensive forts across the north of England which
> remained in use until AD400. The Roman museum
> in the town is worth a detour to discover more.

At the farmyard, turn right, continuing along the
Ribble Way. Continue for 800 metres through a kissing
gate and over a footbridge into the woods, as the river
meanders round to the right.

Before the lagoon, the footpath leaves the riverside
and climbs left through the woods and through a kissing
gate onto open pastureland. Continue along the edge of
the woods then head straight across the field and through
a gate.

After the gate, head slightly left to a signpost on the edge of the coppice, then continue over the stile in corner of the field. Go diagonally over the next field to a gate, then turn right onto the track at **Hey Hurst** and almost immediately left through a gate. Follow the left-hand field boundary as it curves round to reach a footbridge in the corner of the field.

Across the footbridge, follow the path along the woodland on the left for 50 metres, then head half right, diagonally across the field to a stile next to a solitary oak tree. Continue straight over the next field for 250 metres, descending to a stream. Cross the footbridge and follow the path along the edge of the woods for 200 metres before crossing a stile and continuing across field to return to **Lambing Clough Farm**.

Turn left into Lambing Clough Lane and follow it uphill back to the village. At the top of the track, The Shireburn Arms in **Hurst Green** is just 25 metres away on the right.

WALK 23
Longridge Fell

Start/finish	Hurst Green village hall (SD 685 381)
Distance	12km (7½ miles)
Total ascent	290m
Time	3hr 30min
Map	OS Explorer OL41
Refreshments	Millie's Café, Hurst Green

This pleasant circular walk climbs steadily alongside a pretty stream and over fields and farm tracks to reveal a magnificent view out over 'The Shire' before returning via historic Stonyhurst College, where JRR Tolkien wrote part of *The Lord of the Rings*.

Head northwest up Avenue Road, turning left down the footpath just before the de-restriction signs and taking the left-hand track at the fork. Pass the cottages and continue upstream along the river, crossing left via the stone bridge. Continue uphill to emerge from the woods, joining a single track road. Continue climbing west over three stiles and past the reservoir visible through the trees on the right.

After the final metal gate at the top of the track, the path becomes indistinct, but head for a ladder stile over the wall on the skyline to the left of the little knoll. Stay low along the edge of the field to a gate and head right onto the access track to **Huntingdon Hall**, heading northwest up to the main road.

At the main road, turn right for 150 metres before taking the track left towards the kennels. Continue up the track for 800 metres, taking the path on left when the track turns right to the kennels. Continue north for 50 metres then over a stile and on to the open fell. Stick to the field

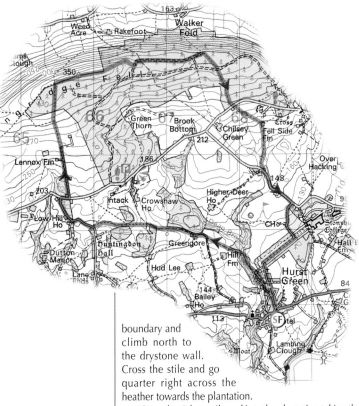

boundary and
climb north to
the drystone wall.
Cross the stile and go
quarter right across the
heather towards the plantation.

Cross the rickety stile and into the plantation taking the
path north. After a couple of hundred metres, you emerge
with a dry stone wall in front of you. Climb the wall and
marvel at the amazing views of Bowland, which dramati-
cally open up before you. Head east on the right side of the
wall to the trig point and summit of **Longridge Fell**.

From here, continue east, crossing the wall via a
new kissing gate and heading back towards the plantation on the left side of the wall. Follow the path into
conifers and descend through the trees, jinking right
before meeting a well-defined track which continues
east again. Ignore the junction with another track after
400 metres, but take the footpath to the right a few hundred metres further on.

Head southeast through the woodland until you reach the road, cross and continue over the wall and diagonally across the field to **Fell Side Farm**. Take the stile into the field and continue downhill towards the wooded gulley and a stile by a gate. Continue downhill, following the stream, through a metal gate past a cottage to join the road. Continue along the road for 400 metres, taking the lane off to the right.

JRR Tolkien stayed at Stonyhurst while his son studied at the college during World War 2. He was working on drafts of *The Lord of the Rings* at the time and some believe parts of the Hodder Valley and Forest of Bowland inspired elements of the vividly described landscape of 'The Shire'.

Follow this lane past the golf course and into the grounds of **Stonyhurst College**. Continue across the grounds to the avenue and follow this right to the Our Lady monument, then follow the driveway through the wood to the top of Avenue Road. Continue along Avenue Road back to the village hall at **Hurst Green**.

The imposing façade of Stonyhurst College

WALK 24
Jeffrey Hill

Start/finish	Little Town Farm car park (SD 609 391)
Distance	11km (7 miles)
Total ascent	300m
Time	3hr
Map	OS Explorer OL41
Refreshments	Little Town Farm Café

This meandering three-hour hike climbs the prominent ridge of Jeffrey Hill, offering expansive views of the Ribble and Hodder Valleys, and passing an ancient inscribed stone said to carry a curse.

The Written Stone

From the car park, follow the footpath through the farm itself between the barns and left of the farmhouse, straight up the track along edge of the field.

Continue on the track, following it round to the left and, at a barn conversion, go left through a small metal gate.

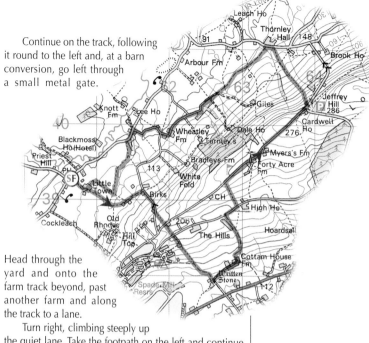

Head through the yard and onto the farm track beyond, past another farm and along the track to a lane.

Turn right, climbing steeply up the quiet lane. Take the footpath on the left and continue climbing beside the wall.

Cross the fence via the stile and continue climbing on the far side to the road. Cross the road and continue over the next two fields to join the track over the lane, descending between the barn conversions before taking the path through a gate and down the field to join the ancient track of Written Stone Lane. Continue downhill along this ancient holloway. Take a right through a gate down a narrow path then through another gate and onto the farm track.

The **Written Stone** – inscribed in the late 17th century, when witchcraft was still a bit of a thing in Lancashire – lies atop a low wall near the entrance to Written Stone Farm. Legend has it that the tenants of the farm had the stone inscribed to

The Bowland Fells from the top of Jeffrey Hill

protect against a local curse, but the stone itself became cursed.

After admiring the **Written Stone**, head back up the farm track and then right along the footpath. Walk through the farmyard at **Cottam House Farm** then take the footpath through gate on the left and continue up the track for 200 metres, taking footpath on left beside a brook. At a gate, continue straight on and through another gate then right up the road for 200 metres before taking a footpath on the left.

The views open out spectacularly, encompassing both the Ribble and Hodder Valleys, Pendle Hill and the Bowland Fells and – on a clear day – Pen-y-ghent, in the Yorkshire Dales.

Go straight along the left field boundary, across the next two fields and right onto a road. Continue along the road for just over one kilometre towards the viewpoint atop **Jeffrey Hill**. ◄

Continue along the road past **Cardwell House** and after the junction, take the footpath on the left, descending steeply and climbing over a stile to the right of a coppice. Continue through the fields towards **Thornley Hall** farmhouse, joining the lane just to the left of the buildings.

Head left down the lane for 100 metres, then take the track off left and follow as it fords a stream and swings back right. Where the track enters a field on the left, continue straight on along the path between the hedges. ▶

After 800 metres, the path joins a lane. Continue straight on, following the road as it meanders to **Wheatley Farm**. After the farm, continue straight down the lane and follow it round to the main road.

Turn left along the main road and walk along the verge for 150 metres before taking the path on the left after a coppice.

Head diagonally across the field then follow a faint path along the stream on the far side of the field to meet a track. Continue along the track for 100 metres then, where the track swings left, take the footpath straight on through the hedge and straight across the field.

In corner of the field, rejoin the track to **Little Town** farm and head right, retracing your earlier route back through the farmyard to the car park.

It can get quite overgrown here, so a stick comes in handy for hacking back the nettles.

Looking north west to the Beasdale Fells

WALK 25
Great Eccleston and St Michael's on Wyre

Start/finish	The Farmers Arms, Great Eccleston (SD 428 401)
Distance	12km (7½ miles)
Total ascent	30m
Time	3hr 30min
Map	OS Explorer 296; Explorer 286
Refreshments	Cartford Inn, Great Eccleston
Public transport	75, 76, 77, 77A from Preston; 42 from Blackpool or Lancaster

The flat, fertile farmlands of West Lancashire are in stark contrast to the rugged hills of the Pennines, and this pleasant riverside walk has plenty of historic interest under the big skies of the Fylde plain.

Parking is limited in **Great Eccleston** and almost non-existent beside the river. Midweek, you may be able to park

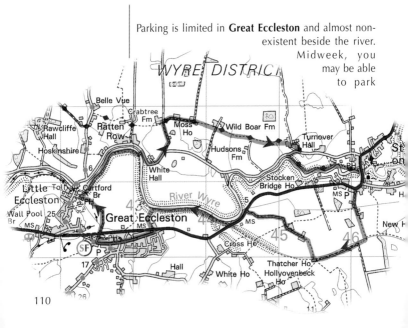

Cartford Bridge

at the excellent Cartford Inn if you check in with the staff and return for lunch or an evening meal. Failing that, find a spot near the public toilets in the centre of the village.

From the village centre, head north onto Butts Lane and cross the main road, then follow the public footpath sign along the track on the opposite side of the road. Cross the stile and go over the field to a footbridge, then over the stile, onto the riverside footpath next to the Cartford Inn.

The **Cartford Bridge** over the River Wyre is a rare example of a toll bridge which continues to be operated by a private limited company. Crossing it on foot is free, but cars pay the princely sum of 20p for the privilege and trucks pay £1 at the toll house on the far bank. Prior to its construction in the 18th century, there was a well-established fording point here and, as its name suggests, the neighbouring 'Cart-Ford' Inn predates the bridge by at least a century.

From the Inn, follow the footpath along the riverbank heading upstream for 800 metres to cross river at a second footbridge and join the lane heading right past **White Hall**. Follow the lane for 300 metres, taking the footpath along a private road on the left. After 250 metres, at **Crabtree Farm**, turn right along track, then, beside some large barns, head slightly left over a paddock and into the fields.

To the northeast, the Bleasdale fells appear on the horizon. Head straight for the grain silo, over the stiles and across the lane, following path for about 800 metres past the ponds to **Turnover Hall**.

Follow the footpath through the farm buildings and past caravans to the lane, then head right for 100 metres to double back left over a stile and onto the riverbank. Continue upstream for 800 metres into **St Michael's on Wyre**.

Cross the bridge and continue on the pavement past the attractive medieval **church** to the footpath on your left. Follow the track for 500 metres past the rather grand house to cross the footbridge over the dyke, then head right along the field boundary and over a stile to join a tarmac track.

St Michael's church

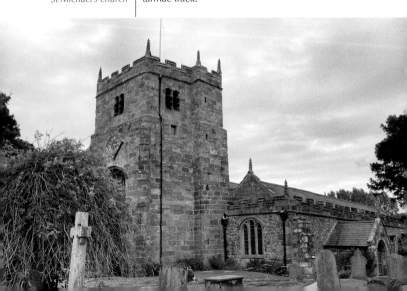

The historic Cartford Inn – a welcoming riverside watering hole

Follow the track into the farmyard then take the footpath off to the right over a footbridge. Continue across a field to a pond, then turn half left through the next farmyard and onto a track.

Continue past the next farm for 500 metres to join the road. Head left along the verge for 200 metres, before crossing to the far side. Turn right over a stile onto the footpath to join the river. From here, you can simply return via the riverbank to the Cartford Inn and then back into the village, or follow this slightly shorter route.

Follow the river for just over a kilometre. At the little coppice, take a footpath on the left to join the main road, heading left again for 50 metres before crossing the road to turn right into Raikes Road. Continue west along Raikes Road to arrive back in the centre of **Great Eccleston**.

WALK 26

Rufford and Mere Sands Wood

Start	St Mary's Marina, just off A59 (SD 464 156)
Distance	9.5km (6 miles)
Total ascent	20m
Time	2hr 30min
Map	OS Explorer 285
Refreshments	The Boathouse Brasserie at the Marina
Public transport	75, 76, 77, 77A from Preston; 42 from Blackpool or Lancaster

An easy-going ramble along the canal and over farmland to a woodland nature reserve, with an option to tie in with a visit to the National Trust's historic Rufford Old Hall.

The Leeds-Liverpool Canal beside Rufford Old Hall

Turn right out of the marina and over the bridge, then turn left to join the towpath along the **Leeds & Liverpool Canal**. Continue north beside the canal passing **Rufford Old Hall** on the left.

Rufford Old Hall is a striking Tudor manor house. Now owned by the National Trust, it was once the family seat of the powerful Hesketh family. Surrounded by pretty gardens, the Hall itself is a treasure trove of Tudor armour, weapons and tapestries, and it's believed that a teenage Shakespeare may have performed in the Great Hall.

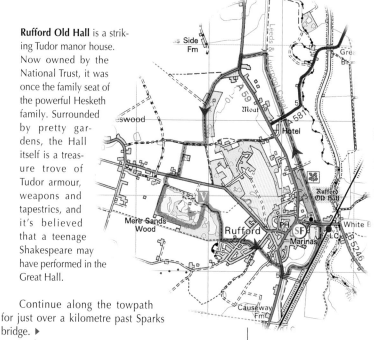

Continue along the towpath for just over a kilometre past Sparks bridge. ▶

At the swing bridge, turn left onto the track and continue to the A59. Follow the road left for 200 metres then cross the busy main road with care beside a coppice, and continue west along Sandy Lane. Follow the lane for 400 metres as it curves gently to the south, through a farmyard and past a house. Take the track on the right where the woodland ends after another 400 metres.

Follow the track west for 300 metres, then follow the footpath left towards a coppice. Continue past the coppice and ponds to the road and follow it right for 150 metres before crossing with care to join the footpath on the left. Follow this path along the field edge and over a footbridge into **Mere Sands Wood** Nature Reserve.

Looking east across the Lancashire plain, the West Pennine Moors emerge on the horizon, with the Bowland Fells brooding to the northeast.

The lakes at the heart of the **Mere Sands Wood** reserve are all that remains of Martin Mere – one of the largest lakes in England until it was drained in the late 17th century. Today it's a well-kept natural oasis operated by Lancashire Wildlife Trust.

Follow the trail around the western edge of the reserve to the **Visitor Centre** (open most days 9.30am–4.30pm). From the Visitor Centre, take the perimeter path back east and follow it along the edge of the reserve towards **Rufford**.

At the gate in the south-eastern corner of the reserve, go left on a footpath along a dyke at the back of a housing estate. Continue past the cricket club then go straight across the road to continue along the path on other side of the dyke.

Cross another road, switching to the left-hand bank of the dyke, and continue along the narrow gravelled path. Cross another road and switch back to the right-hand bank of the dyke, continuing upstream past the depot to meet the A59 at the bridge.

Head right for 75 metres then cross with care and take the track left over the swing bridge and left again onto the towpath heading north. Follow the towpath past the locks back to the marina and across the road bridge to return to the car park at the **Marina**.

The abandoned observation tower

SOUTH LANCASHIRE AND THE WEST PENNINE MOORS

Jubilee Tower (Walk 32)

WALK 27

Barrowford and Foulridge

Start/finish	Car park near Pendle Heritage Centre (SD 862 397)
Distance	11.5km (7¼ miles)
Total ascent	200m
Time	3hr
Map	OS Explorer OL41
Refreshments	Pendle Heritage Centre, New Inn, Foulridge
Public transport	Service 2 from Burnley
Variant	Extension to Foulridge Reservoir, totals 15km (9¼ miles) – about 4hr

This engaging walk connects the fringe of the industrial East Lancashire mill towns with the lovely countryside beyond. Along the way, you'll get great views, industrial heritage, plenty of waterside walking and possibly the odd witch!

Take the footpath running north beside **Pendle Water** upstream for 300 metres, then turn left over the bridge alongside Higherford Mill and continue upstream on a lane along the left bank, leaving the river briefly at the bridge and rejoining after 100 metres.

Continue upstream for 800 metres and cross the footbridge, continuing upstream briefly then taking a gate on the right and climbing to a stile beside a coppice on the skyline.

Cross the stile and continue climbing beside the beck to a gate. Take the next gate immediately on the left and follow the fence, continuing straight on past a farmhouse and through a gate then over the next field to a new housing estate.

Skirt the estate then head right into a lane to meet the main road. Cross the road and go over a stone stile, climbing alongside a fence towards **Blacko Tower**.

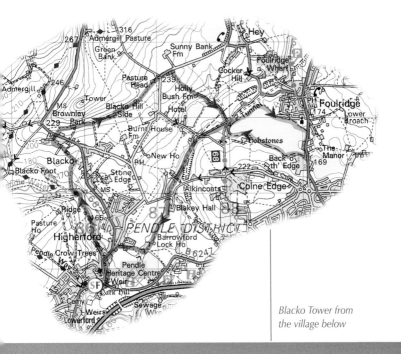

*Blacko Tower from
the village below*

While this prominent landmark may resemble a medieval pele tower, the origins of the **Blacko Tower** are much more recent and have no association with the Pendle Witches. It was built as a folly by local grocer Jonathan Stansfield in 1890 to improve the view.

At a stile, go right along the wall passing to the left of a farmhouse. After another 200 metres, head right over a stone stile and the next field to reach a track. Continue straight on to a farm and through the gates in the farmyard, then slightly left through a garden to a gate into a field. Continue along the edge of the field, following the footpath to Malkin Tower Farm.

Some of the **Pendle Witches** are said to have held their Easter Covern at Malkin Tower on Good Friday, 1612, when all God-fearing folk should have been at church. Local magistrate Roger Nowell saw this as clear evidence of witchcraft and packed the participants off to Lancaster Castle to await trial.

Follow the footpath diversion around the perimeter of the farm then continue across the fields to **Pasture Head Farm**. At the farm, go over the stile and through the gardens to join a track and onto the road.

Continue straight along the road for 200 metres, taking the footpath on the right through Whitemoor Bottom Farm and descend through fields to **Holly Bush Farm**, taking the track heading half left past Sand Hall. At the road, turn right to follow a bridleway signposted Burnley and Nelson.

Extension to Foulridge Reservoir

Alternatively, for a pleasant hour-long extension, cross the road and head through the car park and past the sailing club for a three and a quarter kilometre loop around Lower Foulridge Reservoir.

Main route

After 800 metres, at the road, go left then right, to join the Leeds & Liverpool Canal as it emerges from the Foulridge tunnel, following the left-hand bank.

Continue along the towpath for almost two and a half kilometres, passing under some hump back bridges and a flight of locks until Barrowford reservoir appears on the left. At the lock keeper's cottage, cross the canal via the lock bridge then head half left diagonally across the field to a kissing gate.

Go through the kissing gate and straight on through residential area to road. Head left down to the bridge and return to the car park in **Barrowford** via the riverside path.

Foulridge Lower Reservoir

WALK 28

Holcombe Moor from Ramsbottom

Start/finish	Ramsbottom station (SD 792 168)
Distance	10.5km (6½ miles)
Total ascent	350m
Time	3hr 30min
Map	OS Explorer 287
Refreshments	Ramsbottom is home to a host of bustling bars, cafes and restaurants
Public transport	East Lancashire Railway or 474 and 472 buses from Bury or Bolton

A none-too-demanding hike from the endearingly quirky town of Ramsbottom up onto the moors and back in time for coffee and cake – or a pint – in one of many inviting bars and cafés.

Leave the railway station heading north and cross the road, then turn right across the level crossing and river on the pavement and left along Kenyon Street. The route then runs through an industrial estate for 400 metres. At the end of large recycling plant, turn right onto a path that runs along the backs of some factories then head through a gate and into the fields beyond to join path along the river.

Continue upstream over a footbridge then turn half left along a field edge and through a gate into some woodland. Turn left over a bridge and head along the path running upstream along the far bank to a metal kissing gate.

Head left under a bridge onto a lane. Go under the next bridge as well, then right up the drive and follow it round to the left and through a gate into woodlands. Climb up through the woods for 800 metres then cross the stream and emerge onto the hillside, where views open up to the east.

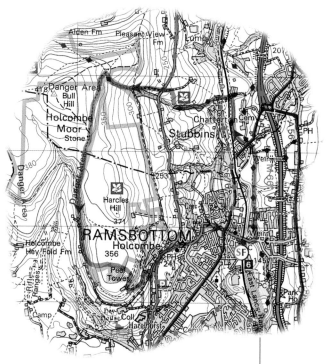

Continue climbing up the left-hand field boundary and cross a rickety stile to continue climbing to go through a gate and onto a track up to the road. Cross this busy road with care and head over the stile and up a grassy path.

Go through a gate and continue uphill following a grassy path round to the right and continue uphill to MOD signs on the edge of the summit plateau.

The site of an ancient **Pilgrims' Cross** atop Holcombe Moor is marked by a more recent monument erected in 1902. The ancient routes of Lancashire were often marked by wayside crosses and it is thought there was a cross on this particular site as far back as the 12th century, when it would have marked the way for pilgrims making for Whalley Abbey.

*The stone marking
the Pilgrim's Cross*

Follow the path south along edge of the summit of **Holcombe Moor**. The path contours gently around to the Tower. At the **Stone** marking the site of the Pilgrims' Cross, continue half right, following marker posts across the plateau and descending over the far side via a rocky path.

The **Peel Monument** is a more recent addition to the landscape – built from local gritstone in 1851 with £1000 raised by public subscription to mark their gratitude to Sir Robert Peel for his role in repealing the Corn Laws. These laws had artificially inflated food prices while depressing demand for the industrial goods produced in the local mills.

Contour around base of the hill for just over a kilometre and when you are opposite some old stone gateposts, take the path left to zigzag steeply back up to the plateau. Head southeast over the plateau to **Peel Monument** and descend right then left via a rocky track to Cross Lane and through **Holcombe** village. Descend into the town via Chapel Lane, go past the church then along Carr Street and Bridge Street back to the station in **Ramsbottom**.

WALK 29

Great Hameldon Hill from Accrington

Start/finish	Church Street, next to war memorial (SD 760 284)
Distance	11.5km (7¼ miles)
Total ascent	330m
Time	3hr 30min
Map	OS Explorer 287
Refreshments	Accrington
Public transport	X41 bus from Manchester
Parking	Arndale Centre is free; numerous free car parks around the station

This town and country trail follows in the footsteps of the Accrington Pals as they prepared to head to the battlefields of the Somme, with route marches and training exercises up on the hills above Hyndburn.

Walk northeast past the market and the bus station and along Burnley Road to St John's church – just 500 metres up the road on an adjacent street off to the left. ▶

Continue up Burnley Road and cross over at a pedestrian crossing to continue southeast along Alice Street, past the school then left up Turkey Street past Peel Park pub, and onto a footpath heading uphill. Follow the track round to the right and continue to zigzag on paths up to the viewpoint.

> This is where a farewell service was held in February 1915 to send off the Accrington Pals battalion to new quarters at Caernarfon.

A **monument** commemorates the donation of this land – now known as The Coppice – to the people of Accrington by William Peel. This is also where the Pals trained before heading to the front in 1915. There's a map on top of the monument to explain the views out over Accrington, over to the West Pennine moors and north to Pendle and the Bowland Fells.

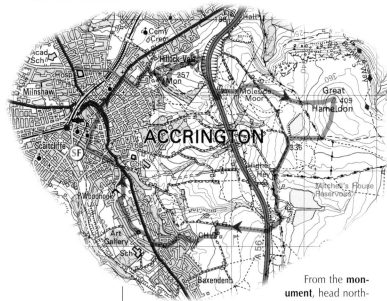

From the **monument**, head northeast along the path then right along the lip of the A56 cutting for 400 metres. Then go through a kissing gate and down to a coppice before heading left through the underpass and up a track. Go left over a stile below

Church Street war memorial

126

the farmhouse and continue over a stone stile onto the hillside.

> Recruited almost exclusively from the town, the **Accrington Pals** were members of a volunteer battalion that suffered terrible losses in the battle of the Somme in July 1916. The principal monuments to the Accrington Pals passed on this walk are in Church Street Gardens and in Oak Hill Park. There is also a room dedicated to their memory in the Town Hall.

Continue past the transmitter then head southeast to the skyline and contour round over **Moleside Moor** to a stile beside a gate in a wall. Cross the stile and follow the track southeast to a bridleway that skirts the summit. Cross the bridleway and head east over a rather boggy section before the final steep climb to reach the summit of **Great Hameldon**.

From the summit trig, descend via the shallower southern slope of Great Hameldon to a wall junction beside May Road Well. Head over the wall, heading west

Horses on Moleside Moor

down a track past the drained reservoir on the right to cross another stile. Then turn left, descending down a wide bridleway to a disused quarry.

Follow the path along the eastern (left hand) perimeter of the quarry onto a tarmac road before joining the road heading right to the A56. Cross the A56 with care and descend west across the fields for 500 metres before taking the path left just after some cottages, towards Meadow Top Farm.

Go through the gate on the right into the field and skirt around the perimeter of farm before heading right again alongside the track on the edge of the golf course. Go left over a stile, round the pond, then left and right to emerge onto Woburn Close.

Descend Waverley Road and turn left onto Southwood Drive, taking the footpath through Laund Clough woodland, emerging onto Laund Road. Continue to the junction then head left along Manchester Road. Cross the road and take the narrow gap in the wall into Haworth Park, climbing past the **Art Gallery**.

Exit from the park onto Hollins Lane and continue north to the gate of Oakhill Park where you will find an impressive stone obelisk, remembering the Pals and the town's fallen in other wars. Continue north to the lower park gate out onto Manchester Road and descend back into **Accrington** town centre via Grange Lane.

The elegant Haworth Gallery overlooks the Pals' memorial in Haworth Park

WALK 30

Anglezarke and Great Hill

Start/finish	Car park at viewpoint overlooking Anglezarke Reservoir (SD 619 163)
Distance	14km (9 miles)
Total ascent	400m
Time	4hr
Map	OS Explorer 285, 287
Refreshments	Accrington
Public transport	125 and 8A from Bolton; 24 from Blackburn

This is one of the most rewarding walks on the West Pennine Moors, offering possibly the best views in Lancashire from the lofty summit of Great Hill.

After parking at the viewpoint above **Anglezarke Reservoir**, walk south down the road and take the footpath on your right, through the car park and down to the reservoir. Head right (north) along the shoreline track for just over three kilometres to the head of the reservoir.

The path climbs away from the head of the reservoir towards White Coppice

At the road go briefly left then right onto a track which leads you up, climbing parallel to the brook. Continue following the brook for 800 metres, then, over the footbridge take the path right, climbing along the lip of the valley. Continue climbing east as the cobbles give way to a well-worn grassy path.

At a junction of paths near the coppice, continue right on a stony path. ◄

Continue past the coppice and up to the summit of **Great Hill** where the views stretch across most of Lancashire and large slices of Greater Manchester, Cheshire, Yorkshire,

By now, on a clear day, Blackpool Tower is visible to the north, while away to the west, the mountains of Snowdonia appear on the horizon.

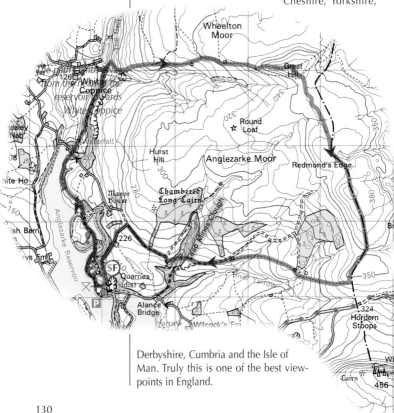

Derbyshire, Cumbria and the Isle of Man. Truly this is one of the best view-points in England.

From the summit shelter, head southeast along a flag-stone path and go right over a stile, continuing along the flags across **Redmond's Edge** towards the transmitter mast on Winter Hill. Head across the dip and up the other side and, after almost two and a half kilometres – 300 metres short of the road – take the footpath on the right.

Follow the path downhill, heading west for 800 metres, and, where it meets a track beside the stream, head right then back left on a grassy track that runs alongside a tumbledown wall. At end of the wall, follow a very faint path across tussock grass heading just north of west and over a footbridge to join a track.

Continue down the track for 500 metres to a wall at SD 633 164, then head right on a faint path and through a kissing gate into some woods. Descend through the trees to cross the stream via a footbridge and climb past mine shafts on the other side to emerge beside a tumble-down wall.

A short 400m detour off to the right beside the plantation brings you to **the Pikestones**. Although they resemble an abandoned quarry working, the Pikestones are the only example in the county of a Neolithic chambered cairn, dating back some 5500 years.

Follow line of the wall to join a track and follow it heading northwest towards the edge of the woods. At Jepson's Gate, descend left on the road for 500 metres back to the **viewpoint car park**.

WALK 31

Belmont and Great Hill

Start/finish	Free car park at Crookfield Road just off A675 (SD 665 191)
Distance	12.5km (7¾ miles)
Total ascent	250m
Time	4hr
Map	OS Explorer 287
Refreshments	Belmont Village
Public transport	535 from Bolton and Blackburn

This easy-to-navigate route showcases the best of the West Pennine Moors, ascending Great Hill from the east. Choose a bright, crisp winter morning to make the most of the truly stupendous views.

From the car park, walk back to the main road, then turn right and after 100 metres cross over and take the track leading through a kissing gate onto access land. Continue west for 400 metres and follow the track as it heads northwest, becoming a boggy sometimes indistinct path across the moorland.

As the path crests a brow at SD 653 190, continue north to drop down into a gulley next to a stand of trees. Cross the wall and head left on path to climb the last 50 metres to reach the top of **Great Hill**. Resist any temptation to cut the corner by taking a direct line across the valley. The going is much tougher than it looks!

From the **cruciform summit shelter**, the views really are stupendous – ranging from Snowdonia to the Lakes and the Isle of Man, to the Sandstone Ridge in Cheshire, the Derbyshire Peak District and the Yorkshire Dales.

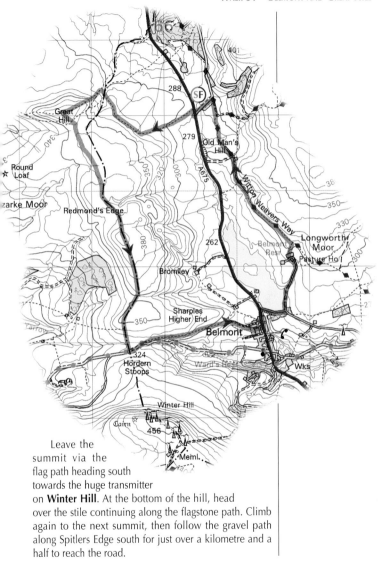

Leave the
summit via the
flag path heading south
towards the huge transmitter
on **Winter Hill**. At the bottom of the hill, head
over the stile continuing along the flagstone path. Climb
again to the next summit, then follow the gravel path
along Spitlers Edge south for just over a kilometre and a
half to reach the road.

133

Peak & Northern Footpaths Society sign on the Witton Weavers' Way

Winter Hill Transmitter is a huge 300-metre mast, 778m (2553ft) above sea level, which makes it the highest point in Lancashire. Constructed in 1965 to broadcast Granada TV, it is the eighth tallest structure in the UK.

Descend left along the road for 200 metres taking the footpath over a stile on the left. Leave access land via a gate and, after 250 metres go right, over the stone stile and follow the track through the gate and into **Belmont**. Here you will find shops and a rather good pub.

Cross the main road with care and head left along the pavement before turning right down the access path to **Belmont Reservoir** and crossing the dam. At the far end of the dam, head left along the track, past the farm building then continue half left through the final farmyard and onto the track of the **Witton Weavers' Way**.

After 150 metres, cross a stile and turn left along the track. Continue along the track for just over three kilometres, past the farm conversion, over the stile and left along the road back to the car park.

WALK 32

Sunnyhurst Wood and Darwen's Jubilee Tower

Start/finish	Small car park off Sunnyhurst Lane (SD 679 224)
Distance	9km (5¾ miles)
Total ascent	330m
Time	3hr
Map	OS Explorer 287
Refreshments	Darwen
Public transport	1, 701 from Bolton and Blackburn

Another exhilarating town-into-country walk on the West Pennine Moors, visiting a monument to local workers who fought for access to recreation up on the moors above Lancashire's mill towns.

From the car park, take the gate in the corner and head downhill into Sunnyhurst Wood, taking the right-hand path at the junction, then joining the main path heading downhill to the valley floor. Follow the path left, past the Greenway shelter, and continue along the footpath alongside the brook. Cross over the footbridge then keep left beside the brook.

At the fishpond, fork right and climb away from the brook, following the path through the woods to the corner of **Earnsdale Reservoir**. Go through a kissing gate and continue straight ahead on the footpath, climbing steeply along a cobble cart track for 250 metres.

At the viewpoint where the gradient levels, continue straight ahead on a gravel bridleway to reach the road. Cross the road and head left along the pavement for 200 metres, before taking the bridleway on the right into the woods and down to **Roddlesworth Reservoir**.

Near the shore, head left (south) on the wide track above the shoreline and continue straight on for 400 metres to cross the first stream, then descend right and

The well house at Hollinshead Hall

cross the second stream on the footbridge. Follow the footpath along the stream and up the steps and continue along the track, through tall stands of beech, before descending the steps to follow the stream once again.

Continue upstream to a gate, then cross the bridge and continue further upstream following the **Witton Weavers' Way**. After a steep climb, continue through the gate and follow the bridleway towards the ruins of Hollinshead Hall and its pretty little well house.

Built by John Hollinshead in 1776 on the site of a substantial farmhouse, the Liverpool Waterworks Corporation subsequently restored the **well house** when building the reservoirs in the early 1900s.

At the distinctive signpost, take path left to Darwen Moor.

At the edge of the woods, cross the road with care and take the track onto the hillside signposted Lyon Den. Stay on the gravel track as it climbs then traverses the summit plateau of **Darwen Hill**. ◀ Follow the track as it winds its way to the **Tower**.

The views open out magnificently to the Ribble estuary and Lancashire coast and across the border into Yorkshire and the Three Peaks.

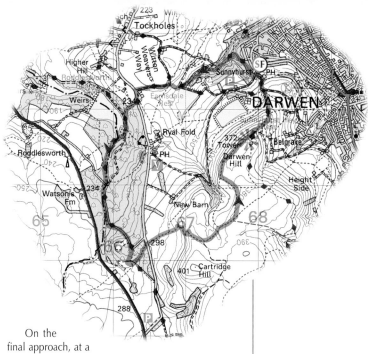

On the final approach, at a fork in the paths, stay on track to the right and follow it to the tower. For those with a head for heights, the views from the top of the tower are outstanding – stretching as far as Snowdonia and the Isle of Man on a clear day.

The **Jubilee Tower** is a celebrated local landmark that was built, not only to commemorate Queen Victoria's Diamond Jubilee, but also to mark the victory of the townsfolk of Darwen in the right of access to the moors. As a precursor to the famous mass trespasses 60 years later, local workers skirmished with gamekeepers over access to the moor, which was eventually granted in 1896.

From the tower, take the gravel path descending northeast (towards Pendle). Follow the track all the way to the road and turn left at the pub to return to the car park in **Darwen**.

WALK 33

The foothills of Pendle from Downham

Start/finish	Car park over bridge on edge of Downham village (SD 785 441)
Distance	8km (5 miles)
Total ascent	250m
Time	3hr
Map	OS Explorer OL41
Refreshments	Downham
Public transport	Service 67 from Clitheroe

This delightful three-hour hike explores the foothills of Pendle, offering extensive views of the Ribble Valley, before diving into the wooded valleys en route back to the picture postcard village of Downham.

From the car park, head for the bridge in the centre of **Downham** village and take the lane forking left before turning right to cross the footbridge to reach the footpath at end of the lane. Go through the kissing gate and follow the path beside the beck, then turn half right to a kissing gate in the top corner of the field (ignoring the stile to the left).

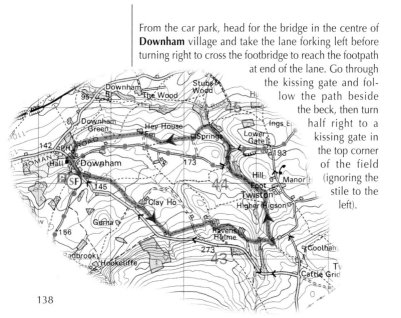

Go through the kissing gate and head right along the field boundary, continuing to climb alongside the fence, with the beck on your left, and over a footbridge. At the farm track leading to **Clay House**, continue straight over and along the field boundary and over a stone stile to Lane Head barn. ▶

Head left across the beck and go straight over the fields. Keeping the post markers across the field on your left, cross the stone stile, continuing straight over the track to Hecklin Farm and along the field boundary. Climb over the stile in the corner of the field, and head for the farm buildings of **Ravens Holme** on the skyline.

Skirt round to the right, above the farm, following the boundary wall to a narrow stone stile. Over the stile, continue straight on and over the track, following the marker stone to another narrow stile. Once over the stile, head along the field boundary to skirt farmhouse to your left, then turn left again to follow the track up the hill for 75 metres. Descend half left along the field boundary down to a kissing gate which leads into the wooded ghyll.

Continue over the footbridge and up the other side of the ghyll, through another kissing gate. The route then climbs steeply across the field, passing to the left of the barn and over a footbridge.

At Brownlow Cottage, turn left then go over a stile beside a gate and follow the fence along the right-hand field boundary. Continue through a gate then through a squeeze stile, following the hedge on the left to a stile in the bottom corner of the field. Over the stile, follow the hedge round to the right and through the gate. Then head half left across the field and through the squeeze stile. Cross the field to a gate to left of **Hill Foot Farm** and go over the stile.

Head half left to follow the field edge to a gate then drop down into the ghyll and past the out barn. Ignore the footbridge on the left and head instead for the kissing gate in the corner of field. Then follow Twiston Beck downstream and through the gate onto a quiet lane.

Continue along the lane for 150 metres then, after the bend, take the footpath on the left before Twiston

Here there are a couple of well-placed benches so you can get your breath back and admire the view back towards Downham from these foothills of Pendle.

The picture postcard village of Downham

Mill. Follow the path downstream beside beck through the kissing gates and left over the footbridge.

> **Downham** was the setting for the classic black and white movie *Whistle down the Wind* where a young Haley Mills starred alongside local children from the village. More recently, it was the location for gentle Sunday evening drama *Born and Bred*.

Follow wall to the cottage then head through the gates between the buildings and right over the stile. Continue to the tree at top of the hill, then over another stile. Continue straight ahead to yet another stile then half right towards the buildings.

Go straight over the farm track and continue along the edge of the fields, keeping straight on the path along the edge of the woodlands. Head across the field for 400 metres before taking the footpath left then right along the lane back to join the road next to the Assheton Arms. Descend the hill then head right down the lane and over the footbridge back to the car park in **Downham**.

WALK 34

Pendle Hill from Pendleton

Start/finish	Car park between pub and Pendleton village hall (SD 755 397)
Distance	15.5km (9½ miles)
Total ascent	520m
Time	4hr 30min
Map	OS Explorer OL41
Refreshments	The Swan with Two Necks, Pendleton

This challenging circuit starts in the pretty village of Pendleton and follows the main ridge to reach the summit trig on the 'Big End' of Pendle. It avoids the increasingly busy honeypot routes to explore the lesser known crags, cloughs and fissures on the less visited slopes of the hill.

Make a donation in the honesty box and from the car park in **Pendleton**, head southeast up the road, taking the track on the right before the church. Go through the squeeze stile to the right of a holiday cottage called The Keep, and continue southeast to cross the footbridge in the top right-hand corner of the field. Continue climbing along the lip of the shallow valley to cross a stile in the corner of the field.

Continue south for a short stretch of about 100 metres, then head left uphill to **Wymondhouses** farmhouse. Go through the gate and over the stile, following the white blobs painted on the trees and crossing the furrows on a faint path up to another gate. Then go left along the track, over a stile and up to the **Nick of Pendle**.

Cross a stile, then follow the road over the Nick and head southeast downhill for 300 metres, before taking the bridleway off to the left before the Cattle Grid. Follow the bridleway northeast for 500 metres to a fingerpost then, when **Churn Clough Reservoir** comes into view continue

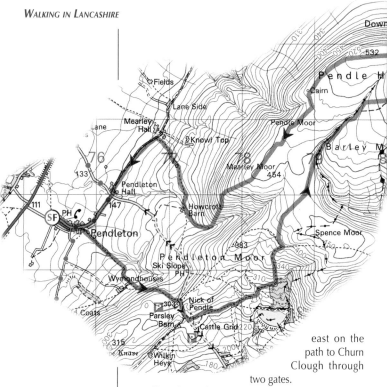

east on the path to Churn Clough through two gates.

Follow the path as it zigzags through the secluded little dell and continue traversing above the reservoir, following the path as it swings north. Ascend steeply up the eroded path to the rugged outcrop of the Deerstones.

At the lip of the Deerstones, head northwest to the wall then go through the kissing gate and follow a faint track north. This then joins the main track along the shallow main ridge. Continue northeast, dropping down to the western lip of Ogden Clough. Follow the path to the head of the clough, then cross the beck onto the summit plateau. Follow the line of 'paving slabs' across the peat to the summit or **Big End** of Pendle Hill.

The steep escarpment and sudden opening-up of the views northeast come as quite a surprise. It's often a windswept and exposed place, but the views are worth the effort – extending over into Yorkshire and the Three Peaks, over the Forest of Bowland and up towards the Lakeland fells on a really clear day.

The paths around the summit have been recently remade as part of a four-year project to improve the landscapes and environment of Pendle Hill. Funded by the Heritage Lottery Fund, this **Pendle Hill Landscape Partnership** project also erected the summit shelter beside the wall.

The view northeast from the summit trig on the 'Big End' of Pendle

143

From the trig point, strike out north to the ladder stile then left, heading west on the path to cross another ladder stile. Contour along the edge of the summit plateau past the shelter to the large memorial **Cairn**, then contour southwest around the top of the clough descending from **Pendle Moor**, aiming for the dilapidated wall visible on the far side of **Mearley Moor**. Use this wall as a handrail to reach the top of Ashendean Clough and your route down.

At the cairn by the corner of the wall, follow the path west down the nose of Ashendean Clough – ignoring the 'tank tracks' to the right. Cross the stream and follow it downstream to join the footpath down the valley to **Howcroft Barn**.

At the barn, cross the footbridge and follow the path to the next barn, then head downhill towards **Mearley Hall**. Cross the beck then go over the stiles and turn left onto the track. Continue to the farm (**Pendleton Hall**), then cross Pendle Road at the staggered junction and follow the quiet lane back into **Pendleton**.

WALK 35

Pendle Hill and the Clarion House

Start/finish	Newchurch in Pendle (SD 823 394)
Distance	10km (6¼ miles)
Total ascent	500m
Time	3hr 30min
Map	OS Explorer OL41
Refreshments	Barley
Public transport	Service 66 from Clitheroe and Nelson
Parking	Limited in Newchurch, so use public transport or park only within the designated spaces on road

This route again avoids the obvious 'tourist' routes up Pendle and instead takes a prettier, quieter route and passes the last remaining Clarion House in England on the way back to the start point.

At the public toilets in the centre of Newchurch in Pendle, take the footpath up some steps climbing to the left of the building. Go through the gate, then left through a second gate and diagonally across the field to reach the stile in the far corner.

Once over the stile, continue to the edge of the wood. Descend to the right on the path along the edge of **Fell Wood** for 300 metres then turn left into the woods. Follow the path to head of the lower **Ogden Reservoir**. Cross the brook and bear right past the Tercet Stone to join the track heading west to the upper reservoir.

Tercet Stones are the distinctive waymarkers that denote **The Lancashire Witches' Way**. They were installed along the long-distance footpath between Lancaster and Clitheroe to mark the 400th anniversary of the Lancashire Witch Trials. Each is inscribed with a poem by the then poet laureate Carol Ann

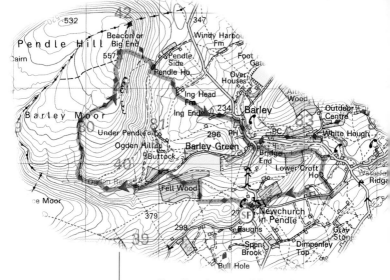

Duffy, telling the story of the witches along the route of their final journey across the moors to meet their fate at the Lancaster Assizes.

Go half left through the gate on the path along the right bank of the upper reservoir and continue up the valley – or clough – as they're known in these parts. At a gate 300 metres beyond the head of the reservoir, go half right and cross the stream to join the well-worn path climbing steeply north.

At the top of the gradient, at the marker stone, keep right and continue climbing steadily as path swings gently northeast. Continue along the grassy path then north on a newly laid path to the summit, or 'Big End' of **Pendle Hill**.

Descend east via 'The Steps' or the 'The Slope' to the gate above **Pendle House**. Follow the path to the right of Pendle House signposted Barley, and descend through the gate. Follow the path for just over one and a half kilometres then head right over the footbridge. At the lane, head right into the centre of **Barley** village, continuing straight over the crossroads then left along **Bridge End** onto a rocky track through the woods.

The Clarion House

Beyond edge of the woods, continue along the track as it descends half right, taking the footpath right over a stile beside a cottage. Head diagonally across the field to a gate and through the farmyard at **Lower Croft House** before turning left onto the farm track to a lane. Turn right and continue along the lane for 300 metres. On the left is Britain's last remaining Clarion House.

Still owned and operated by the local Independent Labour Party, the **Clarion House** is a magnet for local walkers and cyclists to stop off and enjoy a cuppa and a chat with a friendly bunch of like-minded lovers of the great outdoors. Open every Sunday from 10.30am–4pm.

Take the footpath alongside the Clarion House then head left through the gate and through a second gate, then turn right and climb over the stile to cross the next field diagonally to the corner of the wood. Cross the stile and continue through the woods and across the field back into **Newchurch**.

WALK 36

Pleasington and Billinge

Start/finish	Pleasington railway station (SD 642 262)
Distance	11.5km (7 miles)
Total ascent	275m
Time	3hr
Map	OS Explorer OL287
Refreshments	Pleasington
Public transport	Northern Rail from Blackburn

This rewarding 'town-into-country' walk explores the Yellow Hills and the pretty Darwen Valley above Blackburn. Blackburn is famous as the birthplace of Alfred Wainwright, the greatest fell walker of them all.

From the station, head left (north) along Victoria Road for 250 metres and, opposite The Butlers Arms, take the footpath on the right. Follow the path east over farmland and into Witton Park, joining the river beside the bridge after 400 metres. Do not cross the bridge but stay on the left bank and continue upstream through the playing fields beyond the footbridge, then through some scrub across a meadow to the edge of some woods.

At the gate on the edge of the woods, go left, climbing steadily through the woodland to cross a brook. Continue climbing left on the far side, over a farm track then up to the wall at the edge of Billinge Wood. Go through an arch and follow the path climbing steeply northeast through trees to the summit **viewpoint**. ◄

Views have been obscured by new tree growth, but there's a plaque commemorating the court held atop this hill in 1429, where titles to vast landholdings were passed between various local noblemen.

For better views and another commemorative plaque, follow the path descending gently just south of west (left) along the ridge to the edge of the woods. Don't be tempted to take any of the many paths heading steeply downhill, sticking instead to the top of the ridge.

At the edge of the wood, go through the metal kissing gate and straight over the field and over the stile, continuing

southwest over the fields.

On the next knoll, there's a toposcope plaque dedicated to one of Blackburn's most famous sons: Alfred Wainwright. ▶

Before he had the means to get to the Lake District, a youthful **Alfred Wainwright** spent hours tramping the West Pennine Moors above his hometown of Blackburn, where he was an apprentice clerk for the Borough Council. The view of the distant Lakeland fells from the top of Billinge Hill inspired Wainwright to extend his horizons and venture further afield.

Descend to edge of woods and follow the path into the woods before heading left into a lane and then right, signposted **Witton Weavers' Way**. Descend for 50 metres

The views from here stretch as far as Snowdon, Coniston Old Man and Wainwright's beloved Haystacks. On a really clear day, you might even catch a glimpse of Snaefell on the Isle of Man.

The River Darwen at Houghton Bottoms

more through the wood then go half right to cross the open field. Go through a gate into the next field, parallel to the right-hand field boundary. Join the track and continue west, crossing a lane and continuing along the field boundary on the far side. Go through a gateway then cut right through a gap in the hedge and skirt the house onto the lane.

Head left along the lane onto a grassy track then turn half left into the fields. Descend southwest into a wooded valley and out the other side to join the path heading left, alongside a wire fence, descending to the **River Darwen**.

Continue south along the track for 250 metres then head right past the barn. Cross over the footbridge at **Houghton Bottoms** and head right, up the lane. Keep left at the fork and follow the lane then the footpath for a 400 metres under the railway bridge and follow the river upstream, past the **Weir**.

The Wainwright Memorial toposcope

Follow the river upstream for another 500 metres to some woods. Climb right through the woods and over the fields, then head along the track for another 500 metres to join the road. Walk left on the pavement for 400 metres then take the road on the left signposted **Pleasington**. Continue along this road for 800 metres as it meanders back to the station.

WALK 37

Weets Hill from Barnoldswick

Start/finish	Greenber Field locks car park (SD 887 481)
Distance	16km (10 miles)
Total ascent	315m
Time	4hr 30min
Map	OS Explorer OL41
Refreshments	Barnoldswick
Public transport	M5 from Burnley

This engaging route explores the border country where the industrial mill towns of the East Lancashire valleys meet the rich pastureland of Yorkshire.

Leave the car park and follow the path to the canal. Follow the canal south to **Barnoldswick**. After about a kilometre and a half, at bridge 153, cross the road and follow the left bank, continuing south past some factories.

At the next bridge, opposite the marina, leave the towpath to cross the bridge and go through a kissing gate to follow the path uphill, then up a lane past a school. Cross the road and head left then right onto the Pennine Bridleway (PBW), climbing steadily. At the fork, keep left, following the blue marker posts on the PBW. Cross the road and head left then right to continue climbing up the lane. Head left along the bridleway following the marker posts to summit plateau of **White Moor**.

As the track tops out, Blacko Tower comes into view along with the mighty whaleback of Pendle. Continue along the PBW to Gisburn Old Road and turn right. Climb gently towards the summit of **Weets Hill**.

Continue down into the valley and up the other side. The trig point is on access land 400 metres right of lane opposite **Weets House Farm**. Continue ahead, descending the track and admiring views over Pendle, the Ribble

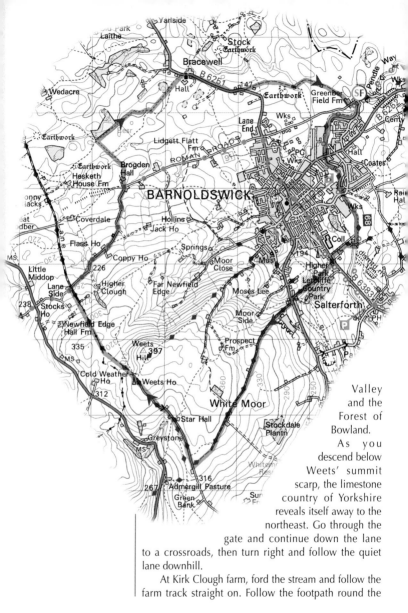

Valley and the Forest of Bowland.

As you descend below Weets' summit scarp, the limestone country of Yorkshire reveals itself away to the northeast. Go through the gate and continue down the lane to a crossroads, then turn right and follow the quiet lane downhill.

At Kirk Clough farm, ford the stream and follow the farm track straight on. Follow the footpath round the

equestrian centre then left over a stile and into fields. Turn half left through a squeeze stile to a footbridge over the beck.

Weets Hill from near Bracewell

Cross the stile above the beck and skirt left around the field boundary to a ladder stile at the corner of a coppice. Follow the green lane right along the edge of the wood. Continue past the **Reservoir** to the end of the wall then carry straight on over the track and half right uphill after the stile.

Head to the next stile and continue along a wire fence over the fields. At the gate, follow the wall left for 200 metres, then go over the stile and past the tennis courts into **Bracewell**. Head right towards the church and continue with care along the road for half a kilometre, taking the bridleway on the left across the fields.

Go through a kissing gate and over the footbridge. Then turn half left to join the track heading through **Greenber Field Farm**, then left along the lane to Greenber Field Bridge.

WALK 38

Whalley Nab

Start	Langho station (SD 705 344)
Finish	Whalley station (SD 730 367)
Distance	7.5km (4¾ miles)
Total ascent	200m
Time	2hr 30min
Map	OS Explorer OL287
Refreshments	Whalley
Public transport	Train from Clitheroe or Blackburn. Trains run every hour from Whalley to Blackburn.
Parking	Park at Whalley and catch train to Langho to start the walk back

This short linear walk starts with a climb up onto a broad ridge, offering superb views of the Ribble Valley, then continues along the ridge to the Nab, above Whalley. It ends with a short, steep descent into this ancient town and its historic abbey.

From the station at **Langho**, head south up Whinney Lane, taking the footpath straight on where the road turns right. Climb up through the woods alongside the stream and over bridges then past a cottage on the right. Go over the stile and join the road coming in from the right, then continue left up the lane to the village at **York**. At the crossroads, go straight on and when the road swings sharply left, continue uphill.

At the crest, continue downhill to the corner of **Dean Clough Reservoir**. Go through a gate to the track on the left that heads downhill to the base of the dam, then go through another gate to join the track climbing to farm track. Turn left, heading east towards Pendle Hill.

Follow the track right through the gate and, at the car park, turn left along the lane, following it past **Sunny**

Bank Farm and a white-washed cottage to reach a stile on left. Climb steeply, crossing a farm track and another stile to reach the top of a grassy scarp.

The path becomes indistinct, but head north to the corner of a conifer plantation.

Cross a stile and follow the less distinct of the two paths through the woods out into a field and across the ladder stile to join the lane, heading right. The views open out on both sides as you continue past an ancient farm to a junction.

Turn left at the junction, past the transmitter and descend the steep slopes of Whalley Nab then up a driveway and follow the path to the right of the cottage at **Nab Side Farm**. Go over the stile and into the field beyond, following the line of a collapsed wall across the hillside. At the end of the wall line, contour round to meet the farm track at the edge of some woodland and take the track right.

Go over the cattle grid and a bridleway joins from the right. Take this path, as it switches back almost the way you came, offering commanding views of Whalley. Keep left when the track forks, continuing steeply downhill until the bridleway turns out onto a track, joining the main road just above the bridge.

The 14th-century gatehouse at Whalley Abbey

Head right over the bridge and into Whalley. Look out for a footpath sign which takes you through a narrow mews and past the Abbey Corn Mill into a new housing development. Cross the courtyard and follow the path past the primary school, turning left when you hit the road to go past the **Abbey**.

Continue under the ancient gatehouse – the oldest remaining part of the abbey – and follow The Sands round to the right and onwards to join Mitton Road just across from the station in **Whalley**.

WALK 39

The reservoirs of Worsthorne Moor

Start/finish	Limestone Trail car park, Long Causeway, Holme Chapel (SD 894 288)
Distance	14km (8¾ miles)
Total ascent	380m
Time	4hr 30min
Map	OS Explorer OL21
Refreshments	The Kettledrum Inn, Red Lees Road, Cliviger
Public transport	592 Burnley to Hebden Bridge

This classic moorland hike traverses a post-industrial landscape and lonely upland reservoirs beneath gnarly gritstone tors. There's a bit of bog-trotting involved, so the confidence to tackle trackless sections is needed.

Park in the car park beside the wind farm and leave the car park through a kissing gate on a grassy trod descending gently northwest to join the Pennine Bridleway (PRW) beside some former quarries. Follow the bridleway through the hills and hollows of these former limestone workings and down Shedden Clough, before heading right at the fork beside the bridge to **Cant Clough Reservoir**.

> The weird landforms in Shedden Clough, known as **The Hushings**, are the end result of an elaborate process of 'hushing' (washing) the limestone out of the hillside. Essentially, the quarrymen built temporary dams and then dismantled them so the water whooshed down the hillside and removed the soil to reveal the limestone, which was then heated in kilns to make quicklime for agriculture and building.

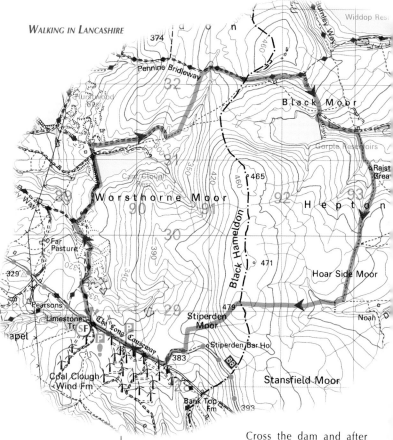

Cross the dam and after another 150 metres, leave the PBW to follow a grassy track heading right over **Worsthorne Moor** to the top of the reservoir. Continue climbing steadily northeast for just over a kilometre to the quarry. Take the footpath off to the left along the far lip of the quarry then right onto the moorland, heading towards the craggy tors of the Hare Stones and Gorple Stones beyond.

Follow the path as it meanders up the valley and rejoins the Pennine Bridleway. Continue right along the bridleway and through the gate above **Gorple Reservoir**. Continue straight ahead to the stones, then descend right on the permissive path along the ridge to the upper reservoir. At the dam, follow the concrete track half left past a plantation and take the footpath right, opposite some sheds.

Cross the stream and climb steadily up Clegg Clough, past the ruined farmstead and continue south up the lip of the Clough onto the open moor. ▶ The bearing for the junction of footpaths on top of Cabin Hill is roughly 174 degrees – just west of south.

On the plateau, continue following a now more distinct path on the same heading for 800 metres. At a wire fence, head right, again following some marker posts to climb along the lip of the valley and over a stile towards Hoof Stones Height. Cross the stile to reach the trig at **479m**, where the panorama extends northwest to Pendle and the Bowland Fells, north to the Three Peaks and southeast to Holme Moss.

From the trig, looking west, descend half left, crossing the sheep fence onto the moorland. Pick up a very faint path that meanders southwest across the tussock grass to a farm gate onto the roadside west of **Stiperden Bar House**. Turn right and follow the road for 800 metres back to the car park.

The path gets very faint here and it's hard going over the tussock grass, but there is the occasional marker post to guide your way.

The gritstone outcrops of the Gorple Stones above the reservoir

WALK 40
Wycoller and Boulsworth Hill

Start/finish	Wycoller pay and display car park (SD 926 395)
Distance	12.5km (7¾ miles)
Total ascent	500m
Time	4hr
Map	OS Explorer OL21
Refreshments	The Old Dairy, Wycoller

The Brontës will forever be associated with the bleak moorlands above Howarth in the West Riding of Yorkshire, but one of the best routes through Brontë country starts in Lancashire.

Follow the path from the northeast corner of the car park east for 500 metres to Wycoller village. Continue past the **Hall** and the Bronze Age Clam Bridge along the track heading southeast, along the **Brontë Way**. After 500 metres, at a three-way junction, take the concessionary path on the right and follow this up through Turnhole Clough to the Bailey Bridge.

Set in the pretty village of the same name, **Wycoller Hall** is said to be the inspiration for Ferndean Manor – Rochester and Jane Eyre's new home after the fire at Thornfield. The ruins of the hall remain impressive, but the history of Wycoller goes back much further. This route passes a medieval pack-horse bridge, a clapper bridge of similar vintage and the striking Clam Bridge, thought to have been constructed in the Bronze Age from a Neolithic standing stone.

Cross the bridge and continue left, climbing steadily above the beck along the Pennine Bridleway for just over

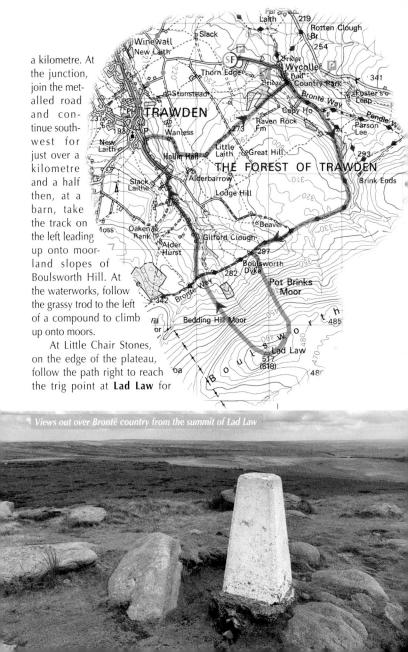

a kilometre. At the junction, join the metalled road and continue southwest for just over a kilometre and a half then, at a barn, take the track on the left leading up onto moorland slopes of Boulsworth Hill. At the waterworks, follow the grassy trod to the left of a compound to climb up onto moors.

At Little Chair Stones, on the edge of the plateau, follow the path right to reach the trig point at **Lad Law** for

Views out over Brontë country from the summit of Lad Law

panoramic views over Lancashire and Yorkshire, stretching from the Bowland Fells to the Holme Moss transmitter.

The moors east of here are known as **Brontë country**. Charlotte and Emily's distinctive brand of moorland misery were shaped by this relentlessly featureless landscape – brutally mundane uplands scoured by wind and rain, frost and ice. Even on the finest spring day, this severe landscape wears a frown.

From the trig point, descend via the steep path down **Bedding Hill Moor**, passing the Abbot Stone en route and crossing the wire fence via a stile to briefly rejoin the Pennine Bridleway.

Turn left and cross the stone stile on the right, walking straight down the field and descending to **Gilford Clough**. Follow the stream along the lip of the clough as it meanders for about a kilometre and a half, joining a track to Meadow Bottom Farm. Then take the path right to join Lanehouse Lane.

Descend left to the cobbled track to a footpath on the right, next to a bungalow driveway, and cross the stile into a field. Continue downhill and cross the stream via the footbridge. Then climb up through the trees and go through the gate of Far Wanless farm and onto the drive then over a cattle grid, taking the footpath left through a gate.

Follow the right-hand field boundary to a gate by the farm, then head left to the next farm. Where the track heads left, keep straight on along the wall to cross a wooden bridge. Go over the stile to another farm and into the woods. Keep straight on, descending into the valley to join the road back to **Wycoller** via the clapper bridge and back to the car park along the road.

APPENDIX A
Route summary table

Walk		Start/finish	Distance	Time	Page
	North Lancashire and the Bowland Fells				
1	Beacon Fell and Brock Valley	Brock Bottom, Claughton (SD 549 431)	8km (5 miles)	3hr	24
2	Bleasdale Ridge circular	Delph Lane, Oakenclough (SD 546 455)	15.5km (9¾ miles)	5hr	27
3	Clougha Pike	Quernmore (SD 526 604)	11.5km (7 miles)	4hr	31
4	Cross of Greet and Bowland Knotts	Cross of Greet Bridge (SD 703 590)	12km (7½ miles)	4hr	34
5	Grizedale and Nicky Nook	Scorton (SD 502 486)	8.5km (5¼ miles)	2hr 30min	37
6	Langden and Hareden Valleys	Near Dunsop Bridge (SD 633 511)	10km (6¼ miles)	3hr	39
7	Parlick Pike and Fair Snape	Near Chipping (SD 602 442)	9.5km (6 miles)	3hr	42
8	Roeburndale – the enchanted valley	Wray (SD 606 675)	11.5km (7¼ miles)	3hr 30min	45
9	Stocks Reservoir circular	Dalehead, near Slaidburn (SD 546 455)	11.5km (6¾ miles)	3hr 30min	48
10	Tarnbrook and the Ward's Stone	Tarnbrook (SD 569 554)	12.5km (7¾ miles)	4hr 30min	51
11	The Upper Wyre Way	Near Tarnbrook (SD 604 538)	12.5km (7¾ miles)	3hr 30min	54
12	Whin Fell and the Brennand Valley	Near Dunsop Bridge (SD 647 505)	11.5km (7¼ miles)	4hr	57
13	Whitendale Hanging Stones	Near Slaidburn (SD 692 547)	15.5km (9½ miles)	5hr	60
14	Whitewell and the Upper Hodder Valley	Whitewell (SD 659 468)	13km (8 miles)	4hr	64

163

Walk		Start/finish	Distance	Time	Page
15	Glasson, Cockersand Abbey and Conder Green	Conder Green (SD 459 559)	13.5km (8¼ miles)	3hr 30min	67
16	Gragareth – Lancashire's county top	Ireby (SD 654 756)	13.5km (8¼ miles)	5hr	71
17	Kirkby Lonsdale and Whittington	Kirkby Lonsdale (SD 611 786)	10km (6¼ miles)	3hr	75
18	Sunderland Point	Overton (SD 433 580)	11km (7 miles)	3hr	78
19	Silverdale and Warton Crag	Silverdale (SD 476 751)	12.5km (7¾ miles)	4hr	81
20	Easington Fell and Beacon Hill from Grindleton	Grindleton (SD 759 455)	12.5km (7¾ miles)	4hr	85
21	The Bowland Traverse				88
	Day 1: Wennington to Slaidburn	Wennington (SD 617 699)/Slaidburn (SD 711 524)	26.5km (16½ miles)	8hr	88
	Day 2: Slaidburn to Giggleswick	Slaidburn (SD 711 524)/Giggleswick (SD 803 629)	19km (12 miles)	6hr	93

West Lancashire

Walk		Start/finish	Distance	Time	Page
22	Hurst Green and Ribchester	Hurst Green (SD 685 379)	8.5km (5¼ miles)	3hr	100
23	Longridge Fell	Hurst Green (SD 685 381)	12km (7½ miles)	3hr 30min	103
24	Jeffrey Hill	Little Town Farm, near Longridge (SD 609 391)	11km (7 miles)	3hr	106
25	Great Eccleston and St Michael's on Wyre	Great Eccleston (SD 428 401)	12km (7½ miles)	3hr 30min	110
26	Rufford and Mere Sands Wood	St Mary's Marina, Rufford (SD 464 156)	9.5km (6 miles)	2hr 30min	114

Walk	Start/finish	Distance	Time	Page
South Lancashire and the West Pennine Moors				
27 Barrowford and Foulridge	Barrowford (SD 862 397)	11.5km (7¼ miles)	3hr	118
variant: include Lower Foulridge Reservoir		15km (9¼ miles)	4hr	
28 Holcombe Moor from Ramsbottom	Ramsbottom (SD 792 168)	10.5km (6½ miles)	3hr 30min	122
29 Great Hameldon Hill from Accrington	Accrington (SD 760 284)	11.5km (7¼ miles)	3hr 30min	125
30 Anglezarke and Great Hill	Anglezarke Reservoir (SD 619 163)	14km (9 miles)	4hr	129
31 Belmont and Great Hill	Near Belmont (SD 665 191)	12.5km (7¾ miles)	4hr	132
32 Sunnyhurst Wood and Darwen's Jubilee Tower	Near Darwen (SD 679 224)	9km (5¾ miles)	3hr	135
33 The foothills of Pendle from Downham	Downham (SD 785 441)	8km (5 miles)	3hr	138
34 Pendle Hill from Pendleton	Pendleton (SD 755 397)	15.5km (9½ miles)	4hr 30min	141
35 Pendle Hill and the Clarion House	Newchurch in Pendle (SD 823 394)	10km (6¼ miles)	3hr 30min	145
36 Pleasington and Billinge	Pleasington, near Blackburn (SD 642 262)	11.5km (7 miles)	3hr	148
37 Weets Hill from Barnoldswick	Near Barnoldswick (SD 887 481)	16km (10 miles)	4hr 30min	151
38 Whalley Nab	Langho station (SD 705 344)/Whalley station (SD 730 367)	7.5km (4¾ miles)	2hr 30min	154
39 The reservoirs of Worsthorne Moor	Near Holme Chapel (SD 894 288)	14km (8¾ miles)	4hr 30min	157
40 Wycoller and Boulsworth Hill	Wycoller (SD 926 395)	12.5km (7¾ miles)	4hr	160

APPENDIX B
Useful contacts

Safety
Mountain Rescue

Call 999, ask for Police then Mountain Rescue

Teams covering this area are Rosendale and Pendle Mountain Rescue and Bowland Pennine Mountain Rescue

Air ambulance
nwaa.net

Travel
Traveline
www.traveline.info

Dalesbus
www.dalesbus.org

Operates tourist services in Forest of Bowland and border with Yorkshire Dales

Car Free Walks
www.carfreewalks.org

Useful resource for walkers who prefer to use public transport

Weather
Mountain Weather Information Service
www.mwis.org.uk

Covers the Forest of Bowland and border with Yorkshire Dales

Met Office
www.metoffice.gov.uk

Visitor information
Visit Lancashire
www.visitlancashire.com

Discover Bowland
www.discoverbowland.uk

Forest of Bowland AONB
www.forestofbowland.com

Arnside and Silverdale AONB
www.arnsidesilverdaleaonb.org.uk

Lancashire Wildlife Trust
www.lancswt.org.uk

Marketing Lancashire
www.marketinglancashire.com

Visit Pendle
www.visitpendle.com

Visit Ribble Valley
www.visitribblevalley.co.uk

Accommodation
Discover Bowland
www.discoverbowland.uk

Marketing Lancashire
www.marketinglancashire.com

Visit Lancashire
www.visitlancashire.com

Walking information
Access Land
www.naturalengland.co.uk
Or search for Natural England at
www.gov.uk

Rights of Way
Lancashire County Council's Rights of
Way Team
tel 01772 530317
prow@lancashire.gov.uk

Cycling
OnYerBike
www.onyerbike.com

eBike Hire
www.ribblevalley-e-bikes.co.uk

NOTES

NOTES

NOTES

NOTES

The Three Men of Gragareth (Walk 16)

DOWNLOAD THE ROUTES
IN GPX FORMAT

All the routes in this guide are available for download from:

www.cicerone.co.uk/1003/GPX

as GPX files. You should be able to load them into most formats of mobile device, whether GPS or smartphone.

When you go to this link, you will be asked for your email address and where you purchased the guide, and have the option to subscribe to the Cicerone e-newsletter.

www.cicerone.co.uk

LISTING OF CICERONE GUIDES

For full information on all our guides,
books and eBooks, visit our website:
www.cicerone.co.uk

CICERONE

Trust Cicerone to guide your next adventure,
wherever it may be around the world...

Discover guides for hiking, mountain walking, backpacking,
trekking, trail running, cycling and mountain biking, ski touring,
climbing and scrambling in Britain, Europe and worldwide.

Connect with Cicerone online and find inspiration.

- buy books and ebooks
- articles, advice and trip reports
- podcasts and live events
- GPX files and updates
- regular newsletter

cicerone.co.uk